Managing Health Sciences Libraries in a Time of Change

MEDICAL LIBRARY ASSOCIATION BOOKS

The Medical Library Association (MLA) publishes state-of-the-art books that enhance health care, support professional development, improve library services, and promote research throughout the world.

MLA books are dynamic resources for librarians in hospitals, medical research practice, corporate libraries, and other settings. These invaluable publications provide medical librarians, health care professionals, and patients with accurate information that can improve outcomes and save lives.

Each MLA book is directly administered from its inception by the MLA Books Panel, composed of MLA members with expertise spanning the breadth of health sciences librarianship.

2023 MLA Books Panel

Members

Heather Jett, AHIP (Chair)
Mayo Clinic Libraries

Susan Maria Harnett, AHIP (Chair Designate)
Nemours Children's Health

Laureen Patricia Cantwell
Colorado Mesa University

Jeannine Creazzo, AHIP
Robert Wood Johnson University Hospital

Amanda Haberstroh, AHIP
East Carolina University

Shanell T. Stephens
University of Maryland, Baltimore

Patricia Ulmer, AHIP
Geisinger Health

Liaisons

Tamara M. Nelson, AHIP (Board Liaison)
University of Tennessee Health Science Center

Stuart Hales (Staff Liaison)
Medical Library Association

Erinn Slanina (Publisher Liaison)
Rowman & Littlefield

About the Medical Library Association

The Medical Library Association is a global, nonprofit educational organization, with a membership of more than 400 institutions and 3,000 professionals in the health information field. Since 1898, MLA has fostered excellence in the professional practice and leadership of health sciences library and information professionals to enhance health care, education, and research throughout the world. MLA educates health information professionals, supports health information research, promotes access to the world's health sciences information, and works to ensure that the best health information is available to all.

Recently Published MLA Books

Assessing Academic Library Performance: A Handbook by Holt Zaugg

Finding Your Seat at the Table: Roles for Librarians on Institutional Regulatory Boards and Committees Edited by Susan M. Harnett and Laureen P. Cantwell

Virtual Services in the Health Sciences Library: A Handbook Edited by Amanda R. Scull

Combating Online Health Misinformation: A Professional's Guide to Helping the Public Edited by Alla Keselman, Catherine Arnott Smith, and Amanda J. Wilson

Piecing Together Systematic Reviews and Other Evidence Syntheses Edited by Margaret J. Foster and Sarah T. Jewell

Accreditation in the Health Sciences: A Handbook for Librarians Edited by Darell Schmick

Essential Leadership Skills for Health Sciences Information Professionals Edited by Janet Crum and Annabelle V. Nuñez

Building Health Sciences Library Collections: A Handbook Edited by Megan Inman and Marlena Rose

Managing Health Sciences Libraries in a Time of Change

EDITED BY

Claire B. Joseph and Priscilla L. Stephenson

ROWMAN & LITTLEFIELD
Lanham • Boulder • New York • London

Published by Rowman & Littlefield
An imprint of The Rowman & Littlefield Publishing Group, Inc.
4501 Forbes Boulevard, Suite 200, Lanham, Maryland 20706
www.rowman.com

86-90 Paul Street, London EC2A 4NE

Copyright © 2024 by The Medical Library Association

All rights reserved. No part of this book may be reproduced in any form or by any electronic or mechanical means, including information storage and retrieval systems, without written permission from the publisher, except by a reviewer who may quote passages in a review.

British Library Cataloguing in Publication Information Available

Library of Congress Cataloging-in-Publication Data

Names: Joseph, Claire B., 1953- editor. | Stephenson, Priscilla L., editor.
Title: Managing health sciences libraries in a time of change / edited by Claire B. Joseph and Priscilla L. Stephenson.
Description: Lanham : Rowman & Littlefield, 2024. | Series: Medical Library Association books | Includes bibliographical references and index. |
Summary: "In Managing Health Sciences Libraries in a Time of Change, experienced leaders of the medical library community offer insights into the current trends and issues faced by health sciences librarians and present practical guidelines and management skills needed to create a culture of excellence" —Provided by publisher.
Identifiers: LCCN 2023048076 (print) | LCCN 2023048077 (ebook) | ISBN 9781538170083 (cloth) | ISBN 9781538170090 (paperback) | ISBN 9781538170106 (epub)
Subjects: LCSH: Medical libraries—Administration. | Medical libraries—United States—Administration. | Medical libraries—Personnel management. | Medical libraries—United States—Personnel management. | Medical librarianship. | Medical librarianship—United States.
Classification: LCC Z675.M4 M247 2024 (print) | LCC Z675.M4 (ebook) | DDC 025.1/9661—dc23/eng/20231220
LC record available at https://lccn.loc.gov/2023048076
LC ebook record available at https://lccn.loc.gov/2023048077

Dedication

To my beloved mother,
Lillian Emmerich Joseph (1920–1995)
My first and best teacher
—Claire B. Joseph

To my sons Giles and Eric, who have been both inspiration and support.
—Priscilla L. Stephenson

Contents

Preface: Managing the Health Sciences Library in a Time of Change — ix

Chapter 1 Overview—The Role of Health Sciences Library Leadership — 1
Melissa De Santis and Gabriel R. Rios

Chapter 2 Trends Shaping Our Libraries — 9
Claire B. Joseph

Chapter 3 Managing Diversity, Equity, Inclusion, and Belonging — 15
Shannon D. Jones

Chapter 4 Staff Support—Leading and Valuing All Library Employees — 35
Katie Prentice

Chapter 5 Leadership vs Management — 43
Gerald (Jerry) Perry

Chapter 6 Management Skills for the Successful Library Leader — 51
Claire B. Joseph

Chapter 7 Mentoring Roles for the Library Manager — 61
Tara Douglas-Williams and Sandra G. Franklin

Chapter 8 Path to Leadership — 75
Rick L. Fought

Chapter 9 Accreditation and Evaluation—Roles for Health Sciences Library Managers — 85
Bethany J. Figg

Chapter 10 Managing the Small Health Sciences Library — 97
Priscilla L. Stephenson

Index — 107
About the Editors — 111
About the Contributors — 113

Preface

MANAGING THE HEALTH SCIENCES LIBRARY IN A TIME OF CHANGE

The opportunity to create this book came at a time for reflection about what it means to be a librarian—particularly a health sciences librarian. Throughout our careers as medical librarians, we have experienced the incredible expansion of online resources and the stress that has been placed on budgets, staffing, and planning. In a short period of time, medical libraries have transformed from collections of print books and journals to databases of digital resources accessible from any desktop. Services no longer must be provided face to face, but the need for virtual services has grown in complexity and now demands a greater knowledge of technology and informatics. Reference service, instruction, cataloging, and collection development all remain as key library tasks, but they have been transformed in this digital environment.

This book will explore what it means to be a leader and manager today. The key is understanding how health science library leaders adapt to change and remain flexible, adapting to outside pressures while maintaining successful library operations. Some medical librarians will be conducting database searches, others will be mentoring new employees, and still others will be members of accreditation or other campus committees. These and other roles are all part of what it means to be a health science librarian today. The successful library manager will be a lifelong learner, refining leadership skills and staying current with trends in librarianship and related professions. This book is designed to serve as a text for students and as a resource for practicing health science librarians seeking suggestions for service improvements. Our hope is that this book will guide readers looking for ways to further develop their management and leadership skills.

1. Overview—The Role of Health Sciences Library Leadership

Melissa De Santis and Gabriel R. Rios

In Chapter 1, Melissa De Santis and Gabriel Rios give us an overview of the role of library leaders. They discuss the responsibilities and role of library leaders from various points of view—including within library departments, on a university campus, and within hospitals and clinical healthcare settings. They have expertise as academic librarians and describe the work of the National Leadership Fellows Program, a joint program of the National Library of Medicine (NLM) and the Association of Academic Health Science Libraries (AAHSL). This innovative year-long mentor program provides training for the future leaders of academic health science libraries.

2. Trends Shaping Our Libraries

Claire B. Joseph

Claire Joseph explores the management trends that are shaping our libraries in Chapter 2. A major shift in university settings has been the realignment of medical school libraries under the umbrellas of their broader university libraries, bringing financial, staffing, and other changes—and challenges—on those campuses. The shift to larger management structures has also been evident in hospitals, where many smaller independent hospitals have merged with large multi-hospital organizations. As a result of mergers and administrative changes, many small health sciences libraries, especially hospital libraries, have all but disappeared. These smaller libraries must fight to survive and to maintain a presence in terms of physical space and staff. They need to continuously demonstrate their value and promote their services to management and users.

3. Managing Diversity, Equity, Inclusion, and Belonging

Shannon D. Jones

In Chapter 3, Shannon Jones provides a discussion of diversity, equity, inclusion, and belonging (DEIB) and explores their importance for successful library management. Library leaders must be cognizant of these issues in hiring and in all aspects of interpersonal relations with staff and library patrons. They should see their management roles as an opportunity to support library staff workers' psychological, physiological, and emotional well-being. Decisions need to be mindful of the concerns of all potential employee groups, student associations, and faculty departments. Managing DEIB efforts effectively begins with commitment from the library's leaders.

4. Staff Support—Leading and Valuing all Library Employees

Katie Prentice

Ensuring staff support is a critical factor of a successful library manager. In Chapter 4, Katie Prentice discusses the human relations aspects of library management—hiring and training staff to ensure a cohesive and supportive group of employees. She discusses recruitment and retention of permanent staff and how to successfully manage all staff—students, interns, permanent staff, and volunteers. The chapter also addresses how to deal with difficult situations and conversations.

5. Leadership vs Management

Gerald (Jerry) Perry

Jerry Perry explores the importance of library management in Chapter 5, demonstrating how it provides the structure for library organization. The successful library manager needs to ensure that day-to-day activities reflect the overall mission of the library while steering the library toward the future with a strategic plan for the next five to ten years. Human resources, space planning, budgeting, marketing, and strategic planning are all important aspects of the library manager's job.

6. Management Skills for the Successful Library Leader

Claire B. Joseph

In Chapter 6, Claire Joseph describes the leadership skills needed to successfully lead libraries. Library leaders need to be able to organize themselves, their staff members, and the work of the library. Time management, project management, decision-making, and emotional intelligence are all critical skills needed by managers. Grant writing and fundraising may be helpful, but all library leaders need to know how to motivate and bring out the best in their employees.

7. Mentoring Roles for the Library Manager

Tara Douglas-Williams and Sandra G. Franklin

Mentoring is a valuable resource that provides staff with a means to develop skills and confidence needed for advancement to new levels of professionalism. Tara Douglas-Williams and Sandra Franklin explore the process of mentoring in Chapter 7 from the viewpoint of both the mentor and the mentee. Both participants in a mentorship must be fully committed to the process—listening, training, and sharing. A successful mentorship will hopefully continue long past the actual end date of a formal program, establishing a life-long collegial relationship.

8. Path to Leadership

Rick L. Fought

In Chapter 8, Rick Fought discusses the path to leadership. For some, this is a sequence of job changes, promotions, and skill development. For others, it can mean becoming an accidental manager, filling in for an absent department head or through an appointment to an interim position. Both paths can lead to permanent positions in a leadership role, although one may have involved more preparation and gradual change.

9. Accreditation and Evaluation—Roles for Health Sciences Library Managers

Bethany J. Figg

Bethany Figg explains accreditation processes and evaluation of library operations in Chapter 9. Evaluation of the library needs to be continuous, although formal accreditation programs bring their own requirements and provide the organization and forms, leaving little to the imagination. Each organization will have its own accrediting agency—and some will have more than one! Hospitals have the familiar Joint Commission (formerly JCAHO) and CARF (the Commission on Accreditation of Rehabilitation Facilities). Universities with medical schools will have the important LCME (Liaison Committee on Medical Education), and most residency programs have their own individual accreditation programs, as well as the Accreditation Council for Graduate Medical Education (ACGME).

10. Managing the Small Health Sciences Library

Priscilla L. Stephenson

In Chapter 10, Priscilla Stephenson examines the management skills needed by librarians in small health sciences libraries. Solo librarians and those with only a few staff assistants face unique challenges as they seek to keep their libraries open each day. They must be capable of research, cataloging, instruction, and collection development. They serve as their own tech support when something goes wrong, and they manage library budgets with often limited funds. These positions require nimble and alert minds that are ready to keep up with developments in librarianship, technology, and the greater world of health science information.

This book explores how health science library leaders face the stresses of day-to-day operations while planning for the future. We hope it will provide useful suggestions for new approaches to library service.

1
Overview—The Role of Health Sciences Library Leadership

Melissa De Santis and Gabriel R. Rios

Key Points

- Although library directors are responsible for the library, they must be involved in and aware of the parent organization's needs. These needs will be different for every organization.
- Library leaders need to allocate more time to strategic work and less time for operational tasks.
- Library leaders need to be able to connect the daily work of the library to the mission and goals of the parent organization. They need to do this work for library staff as well as for their bosses.

Welcome to leadership in health sciences libraries! This chapter will provide an overview of many topics connected to leadership in health sciences libraries. When appropriate, there will be referrals to other chapters in the book that will provide more detail.

Libraries exist as part of a parent organization to support the broader mission of their setting. For health sciences libraries, the parent organization is usually an academic campus or healthcare organization such as a hospital or health system. There is a saying in health sciences librarianship that "If you have seen one health sciences library, you have seen one health sciences library." The cultural, political, and financial environments in which health sciences libraries exist vary widely across institutions. The biggest problems at one health sciences library could be wildly different at another health sciences library, even if the two libraries appear to be very similar on paper. Likewise, even if the problems are the same at two libraries, the most successful solution for each library could vary based on the cultural, political, or financial situation of the parent organization to which the libraries belong. This high level of differentiation requires library leaders to be flexible. It also requires library leaders to use their senses and skills to continually monitor and learn the culture of the parent organizations to which they belong. Chapter 8 will discuss in more detail the skills required of library leaders, such as versatility and the ability to deal with ambiguity. It is the responsibility of the library leader to focus on the larger environment to which the library belongs and to find ways to make connections between the library and its larger environment. Most library staff will be deeply involved in the daily operations and services of the library, which can make it challenging for them to see the bigger picture. A major role for library leaders is to continually state and reinforce the connection between the daily work of the library and how that work supports the mission of the larger environment.

Library leaders should connect with others in the larger environment to look for unmet needs the library could potentially fill. They should track communications in the larger environment that take place through channels such as blog posts, newsletters, or town halls. They should stay current on the impacts to their larger environment coming from outside entities such as accrediting bodies, professional associations, funding agencies, and state legislation. These groups might appear to be removed from librarianship; however, their actions will impact the environments surrounding the libraries. The library will not always be able to assist with managing the impacts that come to their larger environment, but being aware of the concerns that others are facing is an incredible way to support the larger environment.

Library leaders are responsible for both operational and strategic thinking; however, they should expect to focus more on strategic thinking. Operational thinking is focused on the current time period (day-to-day), while strategic thinking is focused on the future. Library leaders need to work with their staff and patrons to create a vision and goals for the library to strive toward, and this requires strategic thinking. The pace of change is constant and continues to increase. The work libraries did ten years ago is different than the work libraries are doing today or the work that will be done ten years from now. A library leader needs to be able to keep their focus on the future to ensure the library will remain a vital piece of the organization.

Types of Institutions and Organizational Politics

Academic

When thinking about health sciences library leadership in an academic setting, the campus will typically have an education mission, a research mission, and a clinical mission. One of the primary responsibilities of a library leader is to determine how their institution emphasizes and approaches each of these missions. There will rarely be an even distribution between the missions. The amount of emphasis given to each mission will affect how resources and support flow within the campus.

At academic health sciences campuses, the capacity needed to support the research and education missions might be larger than the capacity to support the clinical mission. As every campus will be different, it is important to remember that there is no set way for the library to allocate its support to the various missions. For example, some libraries will be heavily involved in the education mission and will play a role in supporting new student orientation, while other libraries might not be involved at all with new student orientation. Directors might personally think it is important for the library to be part of student orientation, but that does not mean they should assume that doing so would be best for the larger environment. In this example, directors need to learn how the student orientation is managed and then decide if there is an institutional advantage for involving the library. Some library staff will have strong feelings if the library is not directly involved with new student orientation; however, staff feelings are not a reason for a library director to advocate for the library to be part of student orientation. That decision should be determined by what is best for the larger institution. The responsibility of the library director is to ascertain where the library can most impact the parent organization and then have conversations with the library staff if the staff needs clarity.

Hospital and Special

Health sciences library leadership often looks different in hospital and special libraries. This is because the mission of these institutions has a different emphasis than the mission at academic institutions. Although there could be an educational component to the mission, the largest and primary mission for hospital libraries will likely be supporting clinical care, and research will usually be the focus for special health science libraries. Libraries in hospital and special settings typically have a smaller number of staff than academic libraries, with many librarians being solo librarians. Because of this, library leaders in clinical settings typically have many operational responsibilities in addition to leadership responsibilities. This is also the case in smaller academic health sciences libraries. Library leaders in these environments often allocate time for core librarian skills in addition to allocating time for leadership responsibilities such as planning, budgeting, and setting a vision. In some ways, it is easier to articulate the organizational mission in a clinical or special setting, but it is also more challenging for a library leader to find the capacity for future-oriented strategic planning.

Politics

The word "politics" gets a bad rap, yet library directors proficient in learning the politics of their parent organization can cultivate strategic importance for the library within their institutions. Every university has its own political environment. Politics may center around competing interests even when the missions are the same or mutually compatible. Colleges or departments might be in competition with each other for funding or committee representation, and each school will also have its own internal politics. Similarly, the academic health sciences center will have its own politics—medical school versus hospital, or possibly other health sciences schools versus the medical school, and so on. Learning the politics of the parent organization can help the library director gain support and resources for staff to do their jobs more effectively and to contribute to the mission and goals of the parent organization.

There is a downside to politics that is often out of our sphere of control. What brings out negative politics is how the personalities of the leaders interact with each other. Politics is a human factor, and the human characteristics—positive or negative—carry over to the institution. The institutional culture takes on the personality of the leader in charge. This applies to all levels of the organization, including the library.

The library is traditionally seen as a neutral entity within an organization; however, being neutral does not mean that the library can sit on the sidelines. The library director should engage with the organization's politics to ensure the resources and needs of the library are recognized.

Roles and Responsibilities to the Institution

As mentioned earlier, when one becomes a library director, the work they will do will be less about the specialized knowledge and skills related to their degree and career (operational) and more about their ability to support the larger organization (strategic). This is true for all library directors whether they work in health sciences, academic, public, or special libraries (Crane 2019; Hernon 2004). Depending on the size of the library staff, the library director may perform very few tasks that are core to librarianship, such as instruction, literature searching, or cataloging. Instead, a library director will be looking for ways the library can demonstrate its commitment to and support of the larger institutional missions. Library directors spend a lot of time listening to and learning about the needs of their stakeholders. To have the capacity to do the work of listening and learning, many of the daily operations of the library are often delegated to other library staff. It is important for library leaders to be aware of the shift in work that will occur when they move into leadership roles. Some might decide they do not want to move into leadership roles if it means they will lose the ability to continue their librarianship practice. When taking on a leadership role, one option to consider is negotiating the ability to continue portions of librarianship practice.

To the library staff, it might appear that once one becomes a library director, they are at the top of the organizational chart. However, because the library exists in a larger environment, there will always be someone above the library director and peers in other units within the institution. This requires library directors to be politically savvy and display high emotional intelligence. It is entirely possible that a library director will have limited authority to make some of the decisions that will have a direct impact on their library, such as determining library hours or when a library should close early due to inclement weather. These can be challenging situations to navigate. In these situations, library directors need to figure out where they have influence and how they can exercise it in a way that best serves the library and the larger institution. Additionally, even when a director has the power to make these decisions, they need to be aware of how their decisions will affect the larger environment, including their organizational peers and their boss. Much of the work of a library director involves their ability to work with other people in productive ways.

For library leaders, there is an impression that one should be doing everything possible to protect the library. This is true to a certain extent; however, library leaders must also consider the larger environment of the institution. There will be times when a goal outside of the library will become a priority for the institution. In these situations, a library leader might make a decision that could be perceived as negative to the library, creating anxiety among the staff. However, the action would likely be beneficial for the institution. A common example in libraries that illustrates this type of situation is when libraries are asked to give up physical space in their buildings to other institutional units. It can be distressing to give up physical space in the library, as this will impact library users and library staff. Library staff and users might perceive the reduction of library space as a reduction in the importance of the library within the institution. The library director is responsible for communicating the reasoning and countering potential negative perceptions by highlighting the greater benefit these changes will bring to the larger institution. Leaders should also help their staff examine their reasons for anxiety; in this case, a decrease in physical space correlates with a decrease in importance. Leaders will often have a chance to negotiate benefits to the library when these situations occur. This means leaders must stay current on library needs so they can make strong requests. As a library leader, one must remember they are part of the leadership of the larger organization, and because of that, they need to always keep the goals and needs of the larger organization at the forefront.

Roles and Responsibilities to the Library

One of the many roles a library director has to the library is strategic planning. Strategic planning in many organizations can cause employees to yawn or think of a retreat away from the office where staff brainstorm about additional work to add to their day-to-day workloads. A small minority of employees may enjoy the process and the energy that strategic planning brings. As a library director, one must set strategic direction for the library and all its resources, including people, services, content, and space. While staff retreats are helpful, they are only as useful as the follow-through and evaluation of impact occurring after the retreat.

Library directors should take a broad view of the organization outside of the library. As mentioned earlier, the library director should learn about the organization outside the library and develop ways to contribute to the parent institution's strategic plan. The library director can create awareness for library staff and demonstrate how each library position contributes to the larger organization.

While strategic planning takes effort, the time spent on reflection and refocusing is worth the cost. As Saunders (2016, 14) noted regarding strategic planning in libraries, "If libraries are not assessing their strategic goals, then they are not establishing their value or holding themselves accountable to their communities." At a minimum, the planning period and follow-up will help ensure that all staff are on the same page about what the library is doing and why they are doing it. The outcomes of the strategic plan also serve as a tool to demonstrate the library's value to administrators and peers.

Influence

All leaders, including library directors, are leading independent people with autonomous minds. One of the skills a library director must master is the ability to influence or inspire others to act on the library's vision. A director can tell library staff exactly what to do; however, most adults do not appreciate being micromanaged. Ultimately, influence allows one to get things done with willing participants. Fairholm (1994, 3) described the collaborative nature of leadership as follows: "Leadership is not a starring role. True leadership describes unified action of leaders and followers (stakeholders) working together to jointly achieve mutual goals. It is collaborative."

Over one's career, the ability to influence will change and grow in different ways. At the beginning of one's career, influence typically means working with other library staff to achieve a common goal. As one ascends into a director position, the audience of influence grows to include peers such as deans of schools, center directors, and other administrators. Using influence at the institutional level requires investment in the long game by planting seeds indicating the role or direction of the library at the institution into the future.

Team Building

Getting people to work as a team means helping them appreciate the differences in their work styles. There are many tools to practice team building, and some of the most useful are inventories and psychological assessments of employee work preferences. These include the Myers–Briggs Type Indicator (MBTI), the DISC, and the Clifton StrengthsFinder. These tools help employees reflect on their personal work preferences and appreciate coworker preferences that might be different from their own. Using these tools to increase awareness among employees can be helpful, and it can be helpful for leaders to review these periodically with their teams.

Two other helpful resources related to team building for library leaders are the Forbes Coaches Council article on high-performing teams (Forbes 2016) and Patrick Lencioni's book on dysfunctional teams (Lencioni 2011). While not specific to libraries, these are great overviews of what is needed to build an effective team.

Recruitment and Retention

Recruiting has been a challenge recently. The pandemic has impacted many of the traditional recruiting and working requirements. Potential candidates expect institutions to provide flexible work policies, including the ability to work remotely and to accommodate nontraditional hours. This is an area where directors may have flexibility, but often that flexibility is dictated by the parent institution. Library leaders need to know the areas where they have flexibility so that they can play to those strengths. They also need to be honest with applicants about where they do not have flexibility.

One key lesson of recruiting is that recruiting motivated people will attract additional motivated people to your organization. It also helps if you hire "happy" people. "Happy," in this context, means people who have a generally positive outlook rather than a tendency to focus on negatives.

To increase retention, leaders must create a culture of transparency, inclusion, and professional development. Transparency is often achieved with consistent communication through whatever channel works best for the library team. There is not a single perfect channel for all locations, and examples of possible methods include in-person meetings, email, chat, Microsoft Teams, or Slack channels. Most of the work of library directors is not confidential and can be shared with library staff. By including staff in library organizational decisions, library staff can directly contribute to the institutional mission. As library staff become more aware of campus-wide or hospital-wide issues, it will help grow their sense of institutional awareness. Professional development is an important perk of an institution. Providing funding and support for career-related development is critical to retaining staff.

Retention is also connected to the broader workplace culture. That broader culture includes DEI (diversity, equity, and inclusion) topics, but it is more than just DEI. Addressing DEI issues as a manager requires real effort, as Elaina Norlin noted: "It is easier to schedule a diversity training than it is to tackle bad leadership, toxic teams, and persistent low morale and distrust" (Norlin 2021, 98). Library leaders must have those necessary but difficult conversations with team members whose behaviors are hurting the library. This does not require punishing those team members, but it does require discussions around behaviors that should be changed to create a more inclusive environment. For more information on DEI, refer to Chapter 3, and for more information on supporting and valuing all library staff, refer to Chapter 4.

Finance and Resource Allocation

The fiscal responsibility of managing a library is clearly important. The fiscal role a director plays is primarily related to understanding how the library's budget functions within the larger environment. Library directors must understand their larger institution's budget model to make prudent decisions about allocating and spending funds. As an example, at some institutions, it is better for the library to overspend its budget rather than have funds left over at the end of the fiscal year. Some institutions require the library to defend their budget every year, which means the library director needs to be prepared for an annual budget justification. Other institutions do not require an annual defense of the library's budget and instead provide the same amount of funds every year. In this scenario, a library director needs to learn the process of requesting additional funds and how that process works. When budgets are tight, the library could be asked to absorb a cut to its budget. The library leader's role is to have a firm understanding of the library's core mission and which services and resources provide primary support to it. The services and resources that provide support for the primary mission will be the ones a library director needs to maintain. It is never easy to make cuts, but leaders must be able to make the cuts that will cause the least negative impact. This can be achieved by focusing efforts on the primary services and resources.

Delegating

A library leader's work involves paying attention to variables outside the library. This might seem counterintuitive because it would seem the library leader should be focusing attention on the library. How can one pay attention both to the library and to the external environment? Typically, the answer is that one cannot do both tasks well, and the library manager needs to delegate some of the library's internal focus to others within the library. This does not mean library leaders do not pay any attention to the library at all. But it does mean they divest themselves from the day-to-day operations of the library and focus primarily on the bigger picture. To do this requires leaders to trust others in the library to manage the details and report back to the director.

Developing Leadership Skills

Library leaders should avail themselves of opportunities for continued learning and development of their leadership skills. One way to do this is by networking with peers. There are two types of peers that library directors should cultivate: institutional peers and consortial peers. For this chapter, we define institutional peers as others within the institution who are outside of the library. They might report to the same boss as the library director, or they might be in a separate part of the institution's organizational chart. They might be higher ranking than the library, the same ranking, or a lower ranking. These are people who can help the library leader stay connected to what is happening at the institution, including conversations that take place outside of meetings or emails. Examples could include the Director of Student Affairs, the Police Chief, the Head of Faculty Affairs, the Director of Institutional Technology, or a Director of Finance and Administration. These peers will not be familiar with library issues, but they will be knowledgeable about the institution's culture and priorities from different points of view. Many times, the missions of institutional peers will be in line with the library's missions, and these peers can provide great opportunities for collaboration.

Consortial peers are other library directors. Examples include directors at other libraries that are part of your institution, directors at other institutions in your state or region, or directors of libraries that the parent organization considers a peer organization. They might be other academic health sciences libraries, hospital libraries, or special libraries. While these peers will not be familiar with the institutional culture of your campus, they will be familiar with library issues in comparable settings. They can provide opportunities to explore how other libraries are working through issues similar to those that your library is addressing. Consortial peers also understand the solitary feelings that library directors experience, as there is typically only one library director at an institution. These peers can be helpful for discussing issues that a director cannot discuss with their internal leadership team.

In addition to peers, there are library leadership programs available that can assist library directors in developing their leadership skills. Examples include the ACRL/Harvard Leadership Institute (https://www.gse.harvard.edu/ppe/program/leadership-institute-academic-librarians) and ARL's Leadership Development & Career Development Program (https://www.arl.org/category/our-priorities/diversity-equity-inclusion/leadership-and-career-development-program/). The NLM/AAHSL Leadership Fellows Program (https://www.aahsl.org/leadershipfellows) is the only leadership program that focuses specifically on health sciences library leadership. The NLM/AAHSL program admitted its first cohort in 2002. The program was developed by the Association of Academic Health Sciences Libraries (AAHSL) following publication of a research report regarding the large number of planned academic health sciences library director retirements (Lipscomb, Martin, and Peay 2009). AAHSL charged a Task Force to create an action plan addressing this upcoming gap in leadership, and one of the products of the Task Force was the Leadership Fellows Program. AAHSL and the National Library of Medicine partnered to fund the program for the first three years. Due to the success of the program, the partnership continues to this day.

The Leadership Fellows Program is a yearlong cohort program. Typically, five fellows are selected, and each is paired with a mentor. Fellows are usually mid-career librarians who are interested in being health sciences library directors and have had some leadership experience. Mentors are current health sciences library directors. Over the course of the year, the curriculum includes a few in-person events, a site visit to the mentor's library, and a virtual curriculum focusing on a variety of leadership topics. Fellows create learning goals and meet regularly with their mentors.

The curriculum of the Fellows Program has adapted and changed based on current issues and trends in health sciences librarianship. This ongoing updating of the content has been helpful and has contributed to the success of the program. Some topics, such as budgeting, power dynamics, and influencing skills, have remained since the first year of the program. Other topics, such as e-science, have been phased out. Diversity and inclusion have always been part of the curriculum, but the amount of time allocated to this topic has increased over the years. The most recent report on the program states that as of December 1, 2021, 52 percent of fellows have received permanent library director appointments.

Continuing Your Journey

Overall, the library director has a role and responsibility to the parent institution. This focus does not minimize the importance of the responsibility to the library staff, but it does recognize that the parent institution must be considered in addition to the library staff when managing the resources of the library. This chapter only scratches the surface of practices, knowledge, and tools contained within these pages that will benefit your leadership journey. Use this book as a guide or a reference tool for reflections as you grow and develop your leadership abilities.

Discussion Questions

1. What are some ideas you have about how one might start to work as part of the institution and less on the day-to-day aspects of the library? What are your thoughts on the challenges of making this shift?
2. Thinking about the missions of education, research, and clinical, what might you do to determine how those missions are prioritized in your current work environment? If you were interviewing for a position at a different organization, what might you do to determine mission priority at that organization?

3. Thinking about strategic planning, what are your ideas about connecting the work done in the library to the larger mission of the institution? Have you seen examples of library directors who have excelled in this area?
4. Have you thought about your continuing professional development as a leader? How might that fit into your overall professional development plans?

Recommended Readings

Hallenbeck, George. 2017. *Lead 4 Success: Learn the Essentials of True Leadership*. Greensboro, NC: Center for Creative Leadership.

Moran, Barbara B., and Claudia J. Morner. 2018. *Library and Information Center Management*, 9th ed. Santa Barbara, CA: Libraries Unlimited.

Works Cited

Crane, Doug. 2019. "Go For It! Advice From Library Directors." *Public Libraries Online*. Accessed August 24, 2022. https://publiclibrariesonline.org/2019/06/go-for-it-advice-from-library-directors/.

Fairholm, Gilbert W. 1994. *Leadership and the Culture of Trust*. Westport, CT: Praeger Publishers.

Forbes Coaches Council. 2016. "13 Characteristics of a High-Performing Team (and How Leaders Can Foster Them)." *Forbes*. Accessed October 30, 2022. https://www.forbes.com/sites/forbescoachescouncil/2016/10/14/13-characteristics-of-a-high-performing-team-and-how-leaders-can-foster-them/.

Hernon, Peter, Ronald R. Powell, and Arthur P. Young. 2004. "Academic Library Directors: What Do They Do?" *College & Research Libraries* 65, no. 6: 538–63.

Lencioni, Patrick M. 2011. *The Five Dysfunctions of a Team: A Leadership Fable*. San Francisco, CA: Jossey-Bass.

Lipscomb, Carolyn E., Elaine R. Martin, and Wayne J. Peay. 2009. "Building the Next Generation of Leaders: The NLM/AAHSL Leadership Fellows Program." *Journal of Library Administration* 49: 847–67.

Norlin, Elaina. 2021. *The Six-Step Guide to Library Worker Engagement*. Chicago, IL: ALA Editions.

Saunders, Laura. 2016. "Room for Improvement: Priorities in Academic Libraries' Strategic Plans." *Journal of Library Administration* 56, no. 1: 1–16, doi:10.1080/01930826.2015.1105029.

2

Trends Shaping Our Libraries

Claire B. Joseph

Key Points

That change is a natural part of life is indisputable. People expect and grow accustomed to changes, large and small, in both their personal and professional lives, and societal and technological changes impact everyone. For years, librarians have been encouraged to be nimble, agile, and resilient, especially when the advent of the internet resulted in a sea change not only in how and where people seek information but also on the value many place on the worth and necessity of librarians, impacting the very existence of health sciences librarians.

However, no amount of nimbleness, agility, or resilience could prepare the world for the once-in-a-century COVID-19 pandemic and its ramifications and repercussions. The life changes from the COVID-19 pandemic brought immeasurable loss to so many and sweeping changes in the workplace. In addition substantial strains on the healthcare system, including hospitals and health systems where health sciences librarians are employed, resulted in very real "change fatigue," or the "overwhelming feelings of stress, exhaustion and burnout associated with rapid and continuous change across healthcare organizations." Nevertheless, "librarians, especially those in the health sciences, are particularly adept at navigating change" (Beaulieu, 454).

Return with Us Now to the Days of Yesteryear

Once upon a time, a library meant only a brick-and-mortar building (or a department in a brick-and-mortar building) where rows of shelves housed collections of actual books and journals. If researchers wanted to know if the library had a specific work in its collection, they used actual card catalogs. To perform a literature search of journal articles, researchers used actual indexes, looking up their subject month by month, year by year.

To read a journal article, students would fill out a form and a library staffer would pull the journal for them; it would either be in paper form, or on microfilm or microfiche, which require loading into a microfilm or microfiche reader. If the researcher needed articles from journals not held by their library, the library would obtain them via interlibrary loan, which would be done by mail (now referred to as "snail mail") or phone. And phones would be what are now referred to as "land lines," as mobile phones, while coming to greater use in the 1980s, were not only what is now referred to as "dumb phones" but were also not in their present convenient, compact shape. (Earliest mobile phones looked something like walkie-talkies). If researchers waited until the very last minute to do their research (which really is "de rigueur" for most students) and couldn't wait for the library to receive their inter-loan, they would have no recourse but to go to the library that did, via car or public transport.

Now Back to the Future

Today's modern library would be unrecognizable with undreamed of resources to, for example, the average baby boomer. Now a library can be entirely digital for both its resources and its professional assistance, and its holdings can be completely accessible remotely. It should be noted that digital resources aren't cheap, and they require not only a reliable power grid but also broadband access for users, not to mention hardware (computers, laptops, smartphones, etc.) to access the information and a dedicated staff to maintain them.

However, while the modern library and its resources make information accessible quickly and conveniently, such convenience has come at a price.

Those born before and educated without the internet have the educational and experiential grounding to know that the source of information must always be ascertained in order to give it gravitas/credence. Ironically, those generations born and educated with the internet have, for the most part, been lulled into something akin to a false sense of security, thinking that "The" internet, or "Dr. Google," is the last word in information. While the internet is an astonishing and truly awesome gateway to vast amounts of information in an instant, something undreamed of by past generations, it is at the same time a platform for any and all to post information, thereby making much information unvetted and possibly incorrect . . . or worse. This pervasive mindset that cuts a wide swath across generations, genders, and socioeconomic groups has, in some instances, drastically diminished the position of the librarian, as some feel there is no longer any need for an intermediary, namely the librarian, as anyone can easily find information on their own. Often the only "intermediary" many require is virtual assistant technology, such as Alexa or Siri.

Perhaps not surprisingly—but still shockingly—this mindset has extended to health care. In fact, the omnipresent internet proved to be something tolling a "death knell" for librarians. "In her Presidential Inaugural Address at the 2013 Annual Meeting of the Medical Library Association in Boston, Dixie Jones shared with her audience that a 532-bed hospital in the United States had recently made the decision to close its health sciences library and lay off the librarian because 'the world-wide Internet has become a main research tool that users can manipulate and navigate without assistance'" (Joseph & Epstein, 69).

The Joint Commission, formerly known as the Joint Commission on Accreditation of Hospitals (JCAHO), policy changes had a great deal to do with this. As Ondrusek and Crow point out:

> "Professional Library Services" was once a discreet category in the Manual (JCAHO 1990, 209-12) but this designation did not survive changes in the accreditation process enacted during the 1990s. JCAHO's evaluation process now centers upon a hospital's ability to carry out "functions"—a term defined by JCAHO as "[a] goal-directed, interrelated series of processes such as continuum of care or management of information" (JCAHO 1999, PF-1). Under these new standards, a hospital librarian's role is defined in terms of "knowledge-based information" directives, an "organizational function" according to the JCAHO accreditation services organizational chart.

In other words, it's not a requirement for a hospital—large or small—to have a library. Add to this the fact that libraries rarely bring in revenue. As Harrow et al. point out, the bottom line is money. "Hospital libraries are not revenue-producing departments, and regardless of our accomplishments and commitment to patient care, they are seen as expendable when budgets are reviewed" (2019, 131).

Health sciences librarians have fought and continue to fight long and hard to get the Joint Commission's attention and persuade them to make a librarian a requirement for a hospital, but this has proven to be something of an exercise in futility. In addition, despite hospital librarians' campaigns using factual arguments, including the return on investment (ROI) profitability metric, many hospital administrators won't or simply can't change their positions.

Of course, all of this is not to suggest all is "gloom and doom," but these changes have impacted health sciences librarians.

Hospital and Healthcare Systems Mergers

Out of financial necessity and the changing landscape of health care, once long-independent hospitals have been forced to look to become part of large healthcare systems, those that often include a medical school or schools of nursing and/or allied health; these systems, in turn, get to expand their reach to other parts of their home cities, into suburban areas, and, at times, to distant states, thus extending their brand beyond their home base. According to Dr. David Grande, Penn LDI Director of Policy, "It's not a new trend but it has rapidly accelerated. There were 1,887 hospital mergers announced between 1998 and the end of 2021, according to the American Hospital Association. Those mergers reduced the number of hospitals from about 8,000 down to around just over 6,000" (Levins). By 2022, two-thirds of community hospitals were system-affiliated.

COVID-19 Pandemic

The "once-in-a-century" COVID-19 pandemic turned the world as we knew it upside down. The disease caused tragic and massive deaths worldwide, and it also affected the day-to-day lives of society at large. Schools of all types were closed, wreaking havoc on the educational system as children, who were now forced to learn remotely, would, in many instances, lose invaluable instruction that would set them back scholastically, not to mention the loss of socialization with their peers, and their participation in organized sports of all types; parents who were still able to work had to seek childcare, an overwhelming task and expense for many; people were forced to "stay at home," thereby losing life-affirming social contacts; and as a result of these "stay-at-home" orders, supermarkets and stores allowed to stay open (as "essential" entities) found products flying off shelves as many did frenzied shopping, leaving entire store aisles stripped bare. COVID-related supply chain issues are still not fully resolved.

The healthcare industry and all who worked in it were pushed well beyond their limits. Scores of patients with COVID-19 were admitted and treated by doctors and nurses, and all workers who were part of the day-to-day operations of healthcare facilities worked endless hours, often at great personal risk, fighting an unknown virus that mutated often. Supplies not only of patient-focused items such as drugs but also personal protective equipment (PPE) of all kinds (e.g., masks, gloves, etc.) were in short supply.

Health sciences libraries and librarians were, of course, not spared. While libraries were increasingly offering electronic resources, including databases, journals, and books, and while some instruction was also offered electronically and, at times, asynchronously, the pandemic nevertheless caused dramatic changes in the day-to-day operations of health sciences libraries. Staff were forced to pivot sharply and quickly, often within forty-eight hours, to close physical spaces and send all staff home to work remotely and maintain a 100 percent online presence in both collections and instructional offerings. Now library leaders were tested as never before, and prayers were said that the library's digital presence was robust enough to maintain the library's offerings. In addition, "The pandemic revealed a digital divide, a gap between employees who have ready access to computers and the Internet at home and those who do not, as well as differences among positions. Remote work is more challenging for employees who must have access to physical resources" (Hosoi, et al., 708). Librarians, of course, were not immune to the many negative aspects of pandemic life, including isolation, lack of socialization, and adjusting to life at home and its impact on family dynamics. And while Zoom and similar platforms proved to be lifelines for meetings and online instruction, as time wore on, many experienced Zoom fatigue.

As the world waited impatiently for life to return to "normal," as Cooper et al. observed, "As additional pandemic waves struck, we quickly determined that a broader framing would be appropriate, as we are not simply in a crisis that will suddenly end but rather experiencing an era" (2022). And as Green astutely observed, "a 'post-pandemic era' may not precisely begin or end during the next several years" (2022, 10). Ultimately, as Albro and McElfresh stated, "The COVID-19 pandemic substantially, and potentially irreversibly, altered work experiences... across geographic and organizational sectors" (2021, 1). After the pandemic major wave was over and COVID-19 became more manageable, society was eager to return to normal, albeit a new normal. The workforce landscape was forever changed, as many positions, including those of librarians, became permanently hybrid.

Of course, libraries have prepared for and been affected by disasters, especially weather-related ones, in the past, including once-in-a-lifetime events like Hurricane Katrina in 2005 in New Orleans, Louisiana; Superstorm Sandy in 2012 in the Northeast United States, which devastated parts of New York and New Jersey; and, in 2017, both Hurricane Harvey in Houston, Texas, and Hurricane Maria in Puerto Rico. All these hurricanes also affected other states and other island nations. As Koos et al. observed, "Prior to the pandemic, most of the attention and discussion on disaster planning revolved around weather and environmental disasters. It took a microscopic-sized virus to shift the conversation" (2021, 76).

Libraries are an integral part of their communities—both geographical and institutional—and don't escape the devastation and turmoil that affects everyone and everything else. And their institutions, be they academic or health care (or both), are also not spared the deplorable and relentless explosion of violence, especially firearm violence, that occurs nationwide.

Yet without diminishing the devastation of these events, it is arguably safe to say that the COVID-19 pandemic resulted in a sea change of societal norms and, at the same time, shone a harsh light on societal inequities, specifically how the underserved of society, most often racial and ethnic minorities, do not have equitable access to health care, resulting in a disproportionate number of deaths and adverse effects from COVID-19.

Society had already shone a harsh light on societal inequities, specifically systemic racism, with the killing of George Floyd in 2020 by a police officer and ensuing equally egregious events. The Medical Library Association and its communities—and other innumerable organizations—issued statements officially condemning systemic racism, violence, and hatred and pledged to support, foster, and nurture diversity, equity, and inclusion.

Diversity, Equity, and Inclusion

We all know the adage "Actions speak louder than words," and this most certainly applies to systemic racism and all its shapes and forms, including healthcare inequities. Many of those same organizations, including the Medical Library Association, that issued statements decrying this blight on our society took *action* in ways large and small to attempt to right these wrongs.

Health sciences libraries and their organizations, be they healthcare systems or colleges or universities, took major steps when they established departments and/or committees of Diversity, Equity, and Inclusion. These departments and their staff seek to chip away at systemic racism, overt and implicit, by inculcating their institutions with compassion, empathy, respect, and understanding for *all*, going beyond cultural competency instruction to cultural humility, empathetic understandings, and respect for all cultures, ethnicities, races, religions, gender-identifications, ages, and disabilities. It is a tall order but "a journey of a thousand miles begins with a single step" (attributed to Chinese philosopher Lao Tzu), and certainly such single steps are long overdue.

The Future of Health Sciences Librarians

Librarians of all types have, historically, been overwhelmingly female and white, and in recent years, "library professionals have never been older" (Green, 3). COVID-19 found that baby boomer retirements "increased at a much faster rate," and many "most likely retired earlier than they would have otherwise." In addition, many libraries have found post-COVID budgetary issues that have, in some cases, impacted staffing and hiring.

A nauseatingly persistent stereotype of the librarian as a stern, dowdy female "shushing" patrons does not help in recruiting new members to the ranks. Historically, librarian was seen as a "woman's profession," one of the few areas where women were permitted or allowed to work, similar to nursing and teaching (baby boomers will have memories of this but not fond ones). When traditionally "men's professions," such as physicians, engineers, lawyers, business executives, and so on, began opening up to women, minorities, and people of color, they were eagerly pursued.

Librarians need to proactively portray their profession in the most positive light possible. And new librarians need to be helped and nurtured in their professional growth. The Medical Library Association offers, along with a wide variety of continuing education, opportunities to find mentorship and experiences and trainings to guide librarians in their careers.

Health sciences librarians, all librarians for that matter, are needed now more than ever. The increasing societal reliance on the internet, Dr. Google, and social media to find health information, often swallowed whole with no thought of its source, was another issue that the pandemic brought under harsh scrutiny. COVID-19 and its treatment options and vaccines let loose a tsunami of misinformation and disinformation to such an extent that the World Health Organization referred to it as an "infodemic." With most turning to the internet and social media (in all its manifestations) to find information, the most unsavory and polarizing viewpoints surfaced, including an increasing and alarming distrust of factual science.

Health literacy is another serious issue facing the general public. According to the Centers for Disease Control and Prevention (CDC), "health literacy is the degree to which individuals have the ability to find, understand, and use information and services to inform health-related decisions and actions for themselves and others." Paradoxically, in this information-rich world, a significant part of the population is medically underserved and truly does not know how to access good health care, let alone where and how to find information. Ironically, they are often the ones who need this information the most.

Change is an inevitable part of life and must be expected to affect all of us, both professionally and personally. Along with all the immeasurable sufferings and hardships of recent years has come the opportunity to shine a light on vitally important societal issues and attempt to right systemic wrongs. Librarians are an integral part of the fabric of society and, as such, will continue to inform, educate, and thereby enrich its patrons.

Discussion Questions

1. How do you envision the future of remote work for health sciences librarians?
2. How can remote instruction and collection access be improved?
3. What actions can health sciences librarians take to mitigate the societal problem of health literacy?
4. How can health sciences librarians help fight the "infodemic" of health information misinformation and disinformation on the internet and social media?
5. What actions can health sciences librarians take to mitigate the problem of fact-based science denial?

Recommended Readings

Lee, Corliss, and Brian Lym, eds. 2022. *Implementing Excellence in Diversity, Equity, and Inclusion: A Handbook for Academic Libraries.* Chicago: ACRL/ALA.
Mroczek, Emily. 2022. *Online Instruction: A Practical Guide for Librarians.* Lanham, MD: Rowman & Littlefield.
Scull, Amanda R., ed. 2022. *Virtual Services in the Health Sciences Library: A Handbook.* Lanham, MD: Rowman & Littlefield.
Virello, Molly. 2022. *Working Remotely: A Practical Guide for Librarians*. Lanham, MD: Rowman & Littlefield.
Weber, Mary Beth, and Melissa DeFino. 2022. *Virtual Technical Services: A Handbook.* Lanham, MD: Rowman & Littlefield.

Works Cited

Albro, Maggie, and Jennesa M. McElfresh. 2021. "Job Engagement and Employee-Organization Relationship Among Academic Librarians in a Modified Work Environment." *The Journal of Academic Librarianship* 47. https://doi.org/10.1016/j.acalib.2021.102413.
American Hospital Association. 2022. "Fast Facts on U.S. Hospitals, 2022." https://www.aha.org/statistics/fast-facts-us-hospitals.
Beaulieu, Lindsay, Cydnee Seneviratne, and Lorelli Nowell. 2023. "Change Fatigue in Nursing: An Integrative Review." *Journal of Advanced Nursing* 79: 454–70.
Centers for Disease Control and Prevention. 2023. "What is Health Literacy?" https://www.cdc.gov/healthliteracy/learn/index.html.
Cooper, Danielle, Catherine Bond Hill, and Roger C. Schonfeld. April 12, 2022. "Aligning the Research Library to Organizational Strategy." ITHAKA S + R: 1-25. https://sr.ithaka.org/publications/aligning-the-research-library-to-organizational-strategy/.
Green, Ashlea. 2022. "Post Covid-19: Expectations for Academic Library Collections, Remote Work, and Resource Description and Discovery Staffing." *The Journal of Academic Librarianship* 48, no. 4. https://doi.org/10.1016/j.acalib.2022.102564.
Harrow, Andrea, Lisa A. Marks, Debra Schneider, Alexander Lyubechansky, Ellen Aaronson, Lynn Kysh, and Molly Harrington. 2019. "Hospital Library Closures and Consolidations: A Case Series." *Journal of the American Medical Association* 107, no. 2: 129–36.
Hosoi, Mihoko, Lauren Reiter, and Diane Zabel. 2021. "Reshaping Perspectives on Flexible Work: The Impact of COVID-19 on Academic Library Management." *Libraries and the Academy* 21, no. 4: 695–713.
Joseph, Claire B. 2018. *The Medical Library Association Guide to Developing Consumer Health Collections.* Lanham, MD: Rowman & Littlefield.
Joseph, C. B., and H. A. B. Epstein. "Proving Your Worth / Adding Your Value." *Journal of Hospital Librarianship* 14, no. 1: 69–79.
Koos, Jessica A., Laurel Scheinfeld, and Christopher Larson. 2021. "Pandemic-Proofing Your Library: Disaster Response and Lessons Learned from COVID-19." *Medical Reference Services Quarterly* 40: 1, 67–78. https://doi.org/10.1080/02763869.2021.1873624.
Levins, Hoag. 2023. "Hospital Consolidation Continues to Boost Costs, Narrow Access, and Impact Care Quality: A Penn LDI Virtual Seminar Unpacks the Challenging Contradictions of this Continuing Trend." https://ldi.upenn.edu/our-work/research-updates/hospital-consolidation-continues-to-boost-costs-narrow-access-and-impact-care-quality.
Ondrusek, Anita, and Suzanne J. Crow. 2002. "The Expanding Domain of Health-Context Video Collections." In Gary P. Handman, ed. *Video Collection Development in Multi-Type Libraries: A Handbook. 2d ed.* Westport, CT: Greenwood Press.

3

Managing Diversity, Equity, Inclusion, and Belonging

Shannon D. Jones

Key Points

- Managing DEIB efforts effectively begins with a commitment from the library's leader.
- The library is likened to an arena, and its leaders are the coaches with their playbook.
- To manage DEIB in libraries, leaders must enter the arena with an open mind and heart, intentionality, courage, a willingness to learn from mistakes, a growth mindset, and a commitment to act.
- Libraries should focus their DEIB efforts on impact, specifically, "How will working for the library affect an individual's psychological, physiological, and emotional well-being?"
- A well-thought-out DEIB playbook is essential. This chapter highlights ten action-oriented plays.

Introduction

In 1910, President Theodore Roosevelt delivered a speech known popularly as "The Man in the Arena," where he said,

> It is not the critic who counts; not the man who points out how the strong man stumbles, or where the doer of deeds could have done them better. The credit belongs to the man who is actually in the arena, whose face is marred by dust and sweat and blood; who strives valiantly; who errs, who comes short again and again, because there is no effort without error and shortcoming; but who does actually strive to do the deeds; who knows the great enthusiasms, the great devotions; who spends himself in a worthy cause; who at the best knows in the end the triumph of high achievement, and who at the worst, if he fails, at least fails while daring greatly, so that his place shall never be with those cold and timid souls who neither know victory nor defeat. (Roosevelt 1910)

The quote resonated with me because being a diversity, equity, inclusion, and belonging (DEIB) practitioner has been worth it, but it has sometimes been challenging. There have been days in the library arena where I felt as if my face was "marred by dust and sweat and blood." Although I strove valiantly, I made mistakes, and I have not yet experienced the triumph of inclusivity in my library workplace. Over time, the quote has encapsulated the mindset necessary for managing DEIB in libraries. Managing DEIB in libraries requires leaders to enter the arena with an open mind and heart, intentionality, and courage and be able to be comfortable while being vulnerable and transparent. In the DEIB arena, the leader needs to be willing to make mistakes, have a growth mindset, and, most importantly, be committed to taking action toward radical inclusivity. Adopting this mindset and enabling action based on it requires much work and commitment. It is a lifelong journey, but each attribute is necessary for entering the DEIB arena.

The arena analogy is plausible for libraries. Consider some typical activities in arenas such as lectures, musical performances, sporting events, and large public gatherings led by a leader who sees the whole playing field. This chapter likens the role of the director to that of an athletic coach who enters an arena prepared to guide their team toward victory using a carefully crafted playbook. The playbook is used to execute game strategies, diagram plays, review player profiles, reinforce team policies, and review previous losses and victories, all aimed at bringing out the best in each player for the greater good of the team. A similar playbook is needed to enter the DEIB arena. Operationalizing DEIB in your library is all about having a strategy and being intentional.

This chapter aims to share insights learned from managing DEIB in an academic health sciences library and is focused exclusively on managing DEIB as it relates to improving the workplace environment for library workers. The chapter begins with a discussion of the role of the library leader and an exploration of how the leader infuses DEIB into the environment. The chapter concludes by sharing tips and strategies for addressing DEIB to benefit library workers at all levels.

Positionality and Guiding Question

This chapter was written with thoughts on how library workers have weathered rising book bans and censorship, the racial awakening of 2020, and the COVID-19 pandemic. The last three years have been traumatic for all library workers, and people have experienced these traumas from various vantage points. As a library leader, this has led me to explore what inclusion looks like in the library arena. Realistically, the library is the primary arena in which I have influence and where I can leverage my privilege as a leader to make that environment a welcoming, safe, affirming, and inclusive space for library workers.

My reflections are based on over twenty years of working in libraries and serving as a library leader who champions positively impacting the work lives of workers in the libraries where I have worked. This chapter is written from my perspective not as an expert in DEIB but as a practitioner who is passionate about the outcomes that become achievable when a diverse group of individuals works to achieve a shared vision or goal. I write this chapter fully aware of the pervasive nature of whiteness in librarianship. At the time of this writing, there were 168,000 librarians and media collections specialists in the United States, with 86 percent identifying as white and 82 percent female (U.S. Bureau of Labor Statistics 2022). These numbers show that significant disparities in gender and race/ethnicity exist in the library workforce. While I am unable at the university level to fully dismantle overall structures and systems that push against libraries being inclusive, I endeavor every day to make my library a great place to work for library workers at all levels.

As an information professional and a library worker, I have always wanted to work in a library where I felt welcomed, safe, valued, seen, heard, affirmed, and included. I wanted to work in a library where I could use my authentic voice, passion, and talent to help the library achieve its mission and strategic goals. This is also the kind of library that I aspire to lead. The question guiding my DEIB work has been, "What impact will working in my library have on an individual's psychological, physiological, and emotional well-being, regardless of their identities?" This question centers on the individual and the unique needs they will need to show up and do their best work. More importantly, using this question for my playbook ensures that I consider what it means to belong in the library environment, regardless of the identities one holds. Since I assumed the library's directorship in 2015, I have thought about what it means to be a leader and what it looks like to provide compassionate care for the library workers I lead. This also motivated me to ponder my "why" as a library leader. My why is rooted in two objectives: 1) to transform library services and support to meet the ever-evolving priorities and information needs of my campus; and 2) to cultivate and sustain a library where library workers can come to do their best work, regardless of the identities they hold. The diversity that library workers bring to their work is a significant part of the library's competitive advantage on your campus.

Definitions

The first step toward creating a more inclusive and welcoming academic library environment is understanding the meaning and significance of diversity, equity, inclusion, and belonging (DEIB). Definitions from the Medical Library Association (MLA) and the Society of Human Resource Management (SHRM) are used to frame this discussion. MLA defines diversity, equity, and inclusion as follows:

- *Diversity* describes the "ways that people are both alike and different; understanding, accepting, and valuing differences that include race and ethnicity, gender and gender identity, sexual orientation, socioeconomic status, political beliefs, language, culture, nationality, age, (dis)ability status, and religion."
- *Equity* "takes differences into account to ensure fair and impartial processes, outcomes, and equal opportunity."
- *Inclusion* means that "all individuals are treated fairly and respectfully; are intentionally valued for their distinctive skills, experiences, and perspectives; have equal access to resources and opportunities; feel a sense of belonging; and can contribute fully to the association's [library's] success." (MLA)

SHRM's definition of belonging captures the essence of what it means to belong. SHRM explains that belonging can be understood as

> having the same feeling at work as you do in a personal setting with friends where you feel comfortable to be there, to share your opinions, to feel truly cared about and accepted, and not afraid to be yourself. (SHRM)

The DEIB playbook requires that leaders fully understand these definitions to ready themselves to enter the arena. An awareness of the arena's customs, rituals, language, rules, and protocols will allow the leader to manage and engage meaningfully as a DEIB practitioner. Vinopal (2016) contends that you will ultimately fail in your DEIB efforts if you are unclear about the goals you are attempting to achieve and why. In the authors' opinion, this failure is a consequence of an unwillingness to identify and examine the factors that prevent change in the DEIB arena. It is common for discussions related to diversity to focus exclusively on race and ethnicity. Though conversations about race and ethnicity are important in libraries, they are not the only dimensions of diversity represented among library workers, and leaders must be aware of the many dimensions of diversity.

Equally important is ensuring that the leader knows the difference between equality and equity since these concepts differ but are frequently used interchangeably. "Equality means that each individual or group of people is given the same resources or opportunities" (Marin Health and Human Services 2021). For example, if you were a leader preparing your team for an upcoming athletic game where you want them to deliver their most impressive performance, you might provide each player with a new pair of size 10 shoes. This would be great for people who wear that size. On the other hand, individuals who do not wear size 10 shoes will receive a resource, opportunity, or support they cannot utilize. Equity "recognizes that each person has different circumstances and allocates the exact resources and opportunities needed to reach an equal outcome" (Marin Health and Human Services 2021). Returning to the shoe analogy, allowing people to pick a pair of shoes in their exact size, preferred color, and style is equity in action. This allows them to engage in the arena in a way that is based on personal choice and comfort.

Entering the Arena, But First . . .

Cultivating an environment where DEIB is interwoven throughout your library program begins with an intentional process of self-discovery at the individual level. Your lived experience significantly impacts how you approach your workday, including how you approach new situations, encounter challenges, find solutions to problems, or establish common ground with others. Accordingly, considering one's frame of reference is essential to managing DEIB. The American Psychology Association (APA) defines a frame of reference as "the set of assumptions or criteria by which a person or group judges ideas, actions, and experiences. A frame of reference can often limit or distort perception, as in the case of prejudice and stereotypes" (APA Dictionary 2023). Our personal frames of reference play an important role in the decisions we make every day in all settings. More importantly, your frame of reference shapes your identity. As a result, it is only possible to discuss managing DEIB by acknowledging the influence of identity.

Influence of Identity

An awareness of how one's identity is developed is an important aspect of managing DEIB. The leader must understand that their own identities inform their adopted worldview. We all have intersecting identities that influence how we see, experience, respond, and interact in the world around us. This exploration is important because these identities impact workplace decisions. We bring these characteristics to every setting or interaction in which we engage. We must consider these things when aiming to cultivate and sustain workplace environments that are welcoming, safe, affirming, and inclusive.

Leaders must be aware of their identities and of those around them. This will assist the leader in providing better professional care for each person they lead. Increased awareness of the identities held will allow you to gain clarity when identifying the influences of power, privilege, and oppression in your environment. This will help you notice when individuals in your environment are marginalized, oppressed, sidelined, or silenced.

I will illustrate how the identities helped to shape my worldview by sharing more about myself. I am a cishet Black woman who uses she/her pronouns. I was raised in a single-parent household with my mother and brother. My mother's extended family supported and nurtured me into adulthood, where I am the youngest of eleven cousins. I came of age in a low-income community in Norfolk, Virginia, where assertive, straightforward communication was required for survival and navigating the community. I was raised as a Christian. I am a Girl Scout troop leader passionate about supporting girls with building courage, confidence, and character. By profession, I am a director of an academic health sciences library, which affords me a middle-class socioeconomic status. I live with two Black men whose well-being I worry about whenever they leave the house. I do not worry about them getting sick at their respective jobs; instead, I worry about them getting stopped by the police and not surviving the encounter. I worry about them being the next Freddie Gray, Philando Castile, Eric Garner, Alton Sterling, or George Floyd. I worry about the very same things for myself. As a Black female, I am just as vulnerable to becoming the next Sandra Bland or Breonna Taylor as my brother and partner. Of all the identities that shape my life and worldview, the intersection of being Black and female impacts me daily.

Identity drives the biases (explicit and implicit) held. Having a heightened awareness of your social and personal identities allows you to disrupt biased narratives you may have about individuals who are different from you. Becoming self-aware requires a deep dive into your own awareness of DEIB issues impacting the world and the people around them. Doing so requires leaders to embrace and respect the unique differences and identities they walk with daily and, more importantly, of those around them. As leaders, we must take intentional steps to disrupt the biased perspectives we hold to be effective in our leadership roles. Therefore, the first strategy I advocate for anyone who wants to manage DEIB in their library successfully is to start at the individual level. Learning more about and acknowledging your blind spots is important in this work. We all have blind spots, regardless of how good we perceive ourselves to be. To uncover your implicit biases, I encourage you to read Mahzarin Banaji and Anthony Greenwald's *Blindspot: The Hidden Biases of Good People* (2016), which has become the definitive guide to understanding how our brains' cognitive processes create implicit or hidden bias, how we can become aware of them, and how we can begin to mitigate against those biases. Follow that reading by taking Harvard's Implicit Association Test (2011), which measures the strength of associations between concepts (e.g., flowers, insects) and evaluations (e.g., good, bad) or stereotypes (e.g., safe, dangerous).

The Responsibility of Privilege

As a leader, you must acknowledge that you have some level of privilege in your life. Many definitions of privilege exist. The one I like best is from Peggy McIntosh's essay, "White Privilege: Unpacking the Invisible Knapsack." McIntosh defines white privilege as

> an invisible package of unearned assets I can count on cashing in daily but about which I was "meant" to remain oblivious. White privilege is like an invisible weightless knapsack of special provisions, maps, passports, codebooks, visas, clothes, tools, and blank checks. (1989, 29)

Another definition comes from Dolly Chugh, who introduced the concept of "ordinary privilege" in *The Person You Mean to Be* (2018a). For Chugh, privilege is ordinary because it blends in with the norms and people around us and, thus, is easily forgotten. The National Association of School Psychologists (NASP) adds, "Privilege can be assigned to populations within a group, such as athletes, individuals perceived as attractive, individuals who attain higher levels of education, or membership in certain religious groups" (NASP 2016). The latter definition illustrates that we all have privileges on some level that impact our decisions at home and in the workplace. However, many people do not like to talk about privilege or get offended when told to "check their privilege."

In the DEIB arena, privilege is a critical issue to address. It is common for DEIB leaders to request people to "check their privilege," which sometimes elicits negative responses from individuals. A request to "check your privilege" should not be construed as a personal attack but rather as a request to pause and consider how privilege impacts your life. As Director of Libraries, I have many privileges, including event invitations, seats at tables, access to information, and influence over library programs. Furthermore, I have access to resources that others may not have because of my socioeconomic status. When the South Carolina Governor sent state workers home to work remotely in March 2020, I incorrectly assumed that all library staff had access to the internet in their homes. This was not the case. When I became aware that some employees lacked home internet access, I had to pause and reflect on my privileges. At that moment, I recognized how my privileges had blinded me to the realities that some employees faced. I encourage anyone in a leadership role to reflect on their privileges. It can be an eye-opening experience.

Bright and Rendón (2021) developed the Privilege Layer Cake (PLC) to facilitate discussions about privilege as an essential component of effective workplace communication. They developed this activity because they recognized that most of us have difficulty discussing privilege meaningfully due to the fear and discomfort surrounding those discussions. However, the topic needs to be discussed. According to Bright and Rendón, conversations about privilege are a crucial first step toward improving workplace environments and improving services for our communities. As part of the activity, Bright and Rendón ask participants to share privileges they had at birth and those they earned over the years. Bright and Rendon Rendón found that the PLC has been a positive way to encourage engagement between people who may not recognize that they share something in common with their colleagues or community members.

Ng (2021) asserts that having privilege does not imply that you are a bad person but instead that the playing field is skewed in your favor. The National Association of School Psychologists (2016) suggests privilege is problematic (a) when it skews our interactions and judgments, as well as (b) when it contributes to or blinds us to systemic barriers for those who do not possess certain privileges, thus creating or perpetuating inequalities. My privilege required me to acknowledge that not everyone has the same access to resources, such as money, food, housing, and the internet, so I need to be inclusive when I make recommendations, establish best practices, and implement policies. To address our internet challenge, we purchased Verizon hotspots for the people who did not have access to the internet at home. To enable people to work from home effectively, we had to fully understand their unique circumstances and establish formal support to assist them.

Chugh (2018b) sees using your ordinary privilege as an opportunity, noting that research repeatedly confirms that those with ordinary privilege have the power to speak up on behalf of those without it and have particularly effective influence when they do. Acknowledging the influence of privilege in your life is essential, but equally important is how you leverage that privilege to support others. A powerful example demonstrating this concept was when Tyler Perry was awarded the Ultimate Icon Award by Black Entertainment Television (BET) in March 2019. In his acceptance speech, he shared a story about helping a person who was blind cross a busy highway (Perry 2019). He used this analogy to discuss the guiding force of his career: to "help somebody cross." Mr. Perry had used his position and privilege to help others "cross," whether bringing his mother from pain to laughter or building his own movie production company to hire Black actors when roles in Hollywood were limited. In these ways and others, he has used his privilege to change people's lives, whether momentarily or long-term. We can do similar actions for the staff we lead.

Questions to consider: 1) What does "helping somebody cross" look like for you? 2) How are you helping people cross? Said differently, how are you using your privilege to support others in your library? My motto for leveraging my privilege to support others is to "lift as I climb." For me, this means nominating library workers for awards on my campus or those offered by a professional association. Ng (2021) offers several examples of how you can use your privilege that aligns with activities that I have done. Those include brokering introductions, being a mentor, being a sponsor, helping others to be seen and heard, and ensuring that personnel at all levels can participate in conversations. Chugh wrote about the ways individuals can use their ordinary privileges that are particularly useful in the DEIB arena:

- Amplifying the views of people not being heard at meetings and bringing back conversations when someone is interrupted.
- Giving credit for people's work and spreading the word about their talent.
- Noticing when bias is playing out around us and naming it when it happens.
- Asking questions, raising issues, and adding perspectives that are not organically emerging in discussions at work.
- Being thoughtful about moments when you may inadvertently speak over the group you mean to support. (Chugh 2018b)

Taking Action in the Arena: A Playbook

Now that we have considered how identity influences our decisions and the power of privilege, let us consider how we can use these concepts to take action in the DEIB arena. Managing DEIB in the library arena requires the leader to act. In this section, I highlight strategies for your playbook. The strategies offered include a variety of practices that you can implement to make your library a more welcoming, safe, and affirming space for your teams.

Building Your Team

Play 1—Practice Self-Reflection

Self-reflection is an important aspect of managing DEIB, as it allows you to examine your biases, assumptions, and privileges. Through self-reflection, you can identify your limitations and work towards becoming a more inclusive and empathetic leader. In addition, it will assist you in fostering a deeper understanding of the experiences and perspectives of others, leading to more effective strategies for promoting diversity and equity within teams and organizations. Consider what inclusion means to you, how you enable it in your sphere of influence, and how it manifests itself in your environment. Your ability to embrace new ideas and perspectives is likely to increase due to this process. Successful management of DEIB requires this kind of personal growth.

Chugh (2018a) suggests the adoption of a growth mindset versus a fixed mindset. In her book, *The Person You Mean to Be*, Chugh takes readers on a journey to see how we can be good people and biased at the same time. She redefines what it means to be a good person as someone trying to be better, as opposed to someone allowing themselves to believe in the illusion that they are always a good person. Chugh also encourages readers to adopt a growth mindset by being willing to learn new information and concepts while having a fixed mind prevents the exploration of new things or experiencing new cultures or perspectives that are different from your own.

Play 2—Assess Your Library's Current DEIB Reality

The leader sets the tone for which people are hired, the library culture, and the level of inclusion that permeates the environment. As a Black information professional, I am in multiple Facebook groups created for library workers who identify as *Black, Indigenous, and People of Color (BIPOC)*, and conversations shared in those groups are a helpful reminder that library environments experience the same toxicity and incivility as other environments. It is possible that your library is not as inclusive as you believe it to be, so for me, managing DEIB begins and ends with the director. You must also have an awareness of "vocational awe" in libraries. Ettarh (2018) coined the term "vocational awe" to refer to the set of ideas, values, and assumptions librarians have about themselves and the profession. These result in beliefs that libraries as institutions are inherently good and sacred and, therefore, beyond critique. Do not let "vocational awe" prevent you from seeing the reality of what it means to belong in your library environment.

Play 2 focuses on acknowledging the reality of the inclusivity in your library, assessing corrective actions you may need to take, and then acting on actionable items. Suggested activities for Play 2 include reviewing:

- The gender, race, and ethnicity demographic of your current workforce;
- The demographic data for your patron population; and
- The demographics of the library workforce in the United States.

Suggested resources to consult include the ALA Member Demographics Study, library employment statistics from the U.S. Bureau of Labor Statistics, and MLA's Diversity and Inclusion Task Force 2019 Survey Report. Comparing national demographic data for library science workers to the demographics of your own library staff will help you identify areas of opportunity when recruiting new personnel. For example, in 2017, all Medical University of South Carolina (MUSC) librarians who identified as male had retired or left the institution to pursue other employment opportunities. Their departure made us aware of the need to correct that demographic gap when we launched our next search. All our recruitment efforts aim to hire candidates with the right combination of experience and education. When we select candidates, we assess their educational background and the knowledge, skills, and abilities (KSA) they would bring to the position. Considering education and KSAs, we determine which candidate will help us strengthen the library's competitive advantage regarding diversity.

Another important action for Play 2 is to review salary information for the new hires compared to your existing personnel. One of the things you want to try to avoid is creating inequities in salary. I emphasize "try," as in reality, this may not be possible due to funding constraints in your environment. However, recognizing where salary inequities exist, understanding why, and looking for opportunities to improve salary equity are actions. The first step in this process is acknowledging that salary inequities have been challenging in libraries for years. Studies calling out the gender wage gap in libraries are not new. A 2022 study by the Institute for Women's Policy Research found that women earned less than men for full-time weekly work in nearly all occupations, including nineteen of the largest twenty occupations for women and all of the largest twenty occupations for men. The group also found that the gender wage gap across racial and ethnic groups is equally profound. ALA's Allied Professional Association notes two types of pay inequities in libraries. The first is pay inequities along gender or racial and ethnic lines, with men earning more than women in the same job with the same experience and education (para 1). The second relates to pay inequality across jobs, such as when public school teachers are paid more than a school librarian with the same education and experience in the same school. What does the salary spread look like in your team? Are inequities present? If so, how might you address those? When preparing for new recruitment or considering salaries, ask the following questions:

1. What is the library's gender and racial/ethnic composition?
2. How do salaries compare to national salary surveys for your region?
3. In what roles do salaries tend to lag?
4. What are the driving factors of the inequities?
5. What barriers exist in terms of addressing inequities?
6. Are these barriers structural or systemic?
7. How might you go about addressing those barriers?
8. Do you have the agency as the library leader to address the inequities?
9. What strategy will you use to inform your team about how salaries are derived?

Your responses to these questions will determine the advocacy needed to address salary inequities in your organization.

Another important step is to see what your employees say about your library environment. Review your employee satisfaction data, if available. MUSC administers several surveys that allow me to capture employees' perspectives on our library environment and my leadership. Those include the Press Ganey Employee Engagement Survey (https://www.pressganey.com/) (administered by the Office of Institutional Effectiveness) and a locally developed leadership survey (administered by the Office of the Provost and the Faculty Senate). Both provide data that speaks to how library workers feel about the environment. Consider what current and former employees say about working for your organization. Two options come to mind. First, you can review exit interview data to uncover themes. In addition, you can check employer websites such as Glassdoor (https://www.glassdoor.com/) and Indeed (https://www.indeed.com/) for comments from current and former employees related to their experiences working for your institution.

Play 3—Recruiting and Retaining Players

Recruitment Strategies

The library's most important resource is its personnel, so Play 3 focuses on building a diverse team. Like coaches, library leaders are pivotal in recruiting their team's best players. Leaders deeply understand their team's needs and the skills required to excel in all the library's functional areas. The library's primary recruitment efforts aim to identify individuals with the desired attributes and potential to contribute to the team's success. Coaches drive successful recruitment, ensuring the library secures the best players and builds a high-caliber team. Recruitment strategies that I have found helpful in my library are:

- Do your homework. Know your library's diversity data. This includes an awareness of happenings in your local community, especially those that make the news.
- Assemble your search committee by considering these questions.
    a. Which library personnel will the person likely work with regularly?
    b. Which non-library personnel will the person work with closely? People in this category are excellent additions for two reasons. First, suppose your library lacks racial and ethnic diversity. In that case, looking for a potential search committee member outside the library is important to demonstrate that the person may find community outside the library. Second, it creates a potential supporter for the new person from day one.
    c. Who on your team has demonstrated a commitment to DEIB?
    d. Who has pushed against it? I caution you from including individuals in this group on search committees.
    e. What training is available to your search committee?
    f. Does your library have required training for search committee members?
- Review the language in your recruitment postings.
- Develop a written advertising and recruitment plan that lists all the places you intend to post your vacancy. You should cast as wide a net as possible.
    a. Post the job announcement in venues where BIPOCs may see the announcement, including free and paid advertisements.
    b. Maintain individual or institutional memberships to professional organizations whose memberships comprise BIPOC professionals, such as the National Associations of Librarians of Color, consisting of the American Indian Library Association (AILA), Asian/Pacific American Librarians Association (APALA), Black Caucus of the American Library Association (BCALA), Chinese American Librarians Association (CALA), and REFORMA: National Association to Promote Library and Information Services to Latinos and the Spanish Speaking.
- Research campus and community resources that may interest prospective applicants to provide a baseline list of resources. Add to the list once you learn more about candidates coming for interviews.
- Plan the interview logistics.
    a. Arrange the candidate's travel and lodging for the interview, as you want to avoid creating financial hardship for the candidate.
    b. During the initial interview phase, ask the candidate if there are campus or community resources they would like to learn more about during their visit. Another strategy is to send a list of resources with the interview packet.
    c. With whom does the interviewee need to meet?
    d. Ask the candidate about dietary restrictions, food sensitivities, or allergies that you need to consider when planning interview meals, as well as any accommodations they might need to be successful during their visit.

Increasing the number of librarians from historically excluded groups has been a goal in library science for decades, yet those numbers still need to catch up. Professional library associations such as the ALA and the Association of Research Libraries (ARL) have made strides toward this priority by creating programs to help recruit people of color into librarianship. Some of these programs have successfully recruited BIPOC students into the profession, yet the number of BIPOCs working in libraries has changed very little. This stagnated growth is just as much a retention problem as recruitment.

Retention is where we lose BIPOC librarians to other disciplines.

Retention Strategies

An important theme threaded through this chapter is the need to foster an environment of belonging and inclusion. To accomplish this, the library should implement diversity strategies and ensure library workers from all backgrounds feel valued, supported, and motivated to stay. Getting people to join the library team is important, but retention is key.

Some practical retention strategies include:

1. Establish a belonging committee or task force to address equity and representation issues.
2. Providing opportunities for library workers to build connections, engage in open dialogue, share their experiences, and contribute to decision-making can help create a sense of ownership and empowerment.
3. Implementing a mentoring program that pairs diverse employees with experienced colleagues can provide guidance, support, and career development opportunities, ultimately increasing job satisfaction and retention.
4. Prioritize workplace wellness by encouraging people to take time off work to reset and don't make them feel bad about doing so.
5. Consider hybrid and remote work options. One of the lessons learned during COVID-19 is that some library functions can be done from remote environments. We also learned that some library workers are sometimes more productive at home due to fewer interruptions. In my library, many staff reported better work-life integration while working remotely. At the time of this writing, my library's leadership team is exploring what a hybrid work arrangement will mean for all levels of staff in our environment. The guiding principle is to balance being present on campus, meeting our patron's needs, and affording the staff the work-life integration they need to succeed.

An incredibly effective retention strategy your library can pursue is prioritizing and supporting professional development opportunities for all library workers, regardless of their background or role. By offering financial support and release time for attendance at local, regional, and national conferences, workshops, and networking events, libraries can effectively promote continuous learning and growth among their staff. This is especially important for library workers from historically excluded backgrounds, such as women and people from various racial and ethnic backgrounds who have often been passed over for such opportunities.

Attending conferences, workshops, and networking events provides library personnel with valuable opportunities to enhance their skills, expand their knowledge, and stay abreast of industry trends and best practices. By investing in the professional development of library workers, libraries can foster a culture of continuous learning and ensure staff have diverse skill sets to support the library program. According to LinkedIn Learning's *2018 Workplace Learning Report*, 94 percent of employees said they would stay longer at a company that invested in their careers.

Supporting professional development for all library personnel, regardless of background or functional role, is crucial for maintaining a skilled and engaged workforce. It benefits individual staff members and contributes to the overall success and effectiveness of the library program. By investing in continuous growth and learning, libraries commit to professional advancement and create a positive and supportive work environment. Other strategies that I have found helpful include:

1. Embrace their lived experiences.
2. Believe them when they tell you something in the environment is not working.

3. Acknowledge BIPOC contributions and celebrate their successes.
4. Offer BIPOCs competitive, equitable compensation.
5. Encourage internal and external mentorship.
6. Learn to pronounce people's names correctly.
7. Encourage them to pursue promotion and tenure and support them to do so.

Play 4—Asking People What They Need to Be Successful

The most powerful question you can ask your team members is what they need to succeed. Richard Finnegan encourages leaders to implement "stay interviews," which he defines as "a structured discussion a leader conducts with an individual employee to learn specific actions the leader can take to strengthen the employee's engagement and retention with the organization" (Finnegan 2018). This will allow the individual to tell the leader what support or resources they need to be successful in the library. Finnegan also shares that stay interviews should be conducted in a one-on-one setting so that solutions are personal to avoid the trap of designing group solutions. When implemented right, Finnegan says some of the benefits of stay interviews include that they allow the employee to hear directly from their supervisor that they care and want the employee to stay and grow with the library, situating the responsibility for employee retention and engagement with the supervisor and building trust in the leader/employee relationship. Liu (2021) adds that stay interviews allow leaders to ask employees why they stay, what could be better about their work experience, and how they envision the next stage of their career within the organization.

Play 5—Inviting a Diverse Group of People to the Decision-Making Table

In a 2014 article for *Scientific American*, Katherine Phillips asserted that diversity makes us smarter because we learn from the ways we are different. Today's libraries are complex organizations trying to meet the evolving needs of the constituents being served. Finding solutions to these challenges requires the library to have a diverse set of individuals at decision-making tables to help solve challenges that we are facing in our libraries, and to drive discoveries and innovation is important for our libraries and the clientele we serve. If you assemble a group and include only one type of employee group, you have failed the inclusivity assignment and are likely sitting in an echo chamber. An echo chamber is "an environment in which a person encounters only beliefs or opinions that coincide with their own, so that their existing views are reinforced, and alternative ideas are not considered" (Dictionary.com n.d.).

You need library workers from all levels in your library sitting at the table to offer suggestions based on their vantage points. In no way should I, as the library director, be telling the staff who work at the front desk how to do their work or telling librarians how to do instruction. I am not close enough to that work at this point. People closest to the work should advise you on possible solutions.

Play 6—Engaging in Critical Conversations Thoughtfully and Authentically

Play 6 is about seeing the humanity in others. Recognizing another person's humanity starts with a conversation. You can appreciate the lived experiences of people whose identities differ from yours only if you are willing to move beyond your comfort zone when broaching DEIB topics. Regardless of the setting, conversations on DEIB can be difficult, but these conversations are necessary for managing DEIB in your library.

To begin, you must set the stage for conversations on DEIB topics. The American Association of University Women (AAUW) offers tools leaders may use to make DEIB conversations meaningful and productive. AAUW posits that setting ground rules for those engaging in DEIB conversations is the most important step. It is also noted that participants should assist with developing the ground rules. An infographic from *Catalyst* (2016) offers seven ground rules you can use in conversations with colleagues, in a team, or in large group settings:

- Assume positive intent.
- Engage in dialogue, not debate.
- Hold yourself and others accountable for demonstrating cultural humility.
- Be open, transparent, and willing to admit mistakes.
- Embrace the power of humble listening.
- Create trusting and safe spaces—where a little bit of discomfort is okay.
- Commit to having conversations that matter by speaking up to bridge divides.

Your aim should be "to create a forum for open and productive discussions where people feel safe sharing their experiences and perspectives and are receptive to learning" (*Catalyst* 2016).

The AAUW champions community agreements when engaging in group conversations about DEIB (AAUW n.d.). Community agreements are useful for ensuring the space feels safe for conversation and exploration. Community agreements allow the group to agree on certain ground rules and promise to honor and respect everyone's thoughts, ideas, and opinions for each session. GLSEN's "Guidelines for Respectful GSA Spaces" provides a useful checklist that I have found helpful in my DEIB work (https://www.glsen.org/activity/guidelines-respectful-gsa-spaces). Regardless of the source, community agreements and guidelines are important, especially when engaging BIPOC and other individuals from historically excluded groups.

Another helpful strategy is to ask BIPOC library workers or individuals from historically excluded groups about their experience in your library environment. Special care and consideration must be taken when engaging library workers who are BIPOC or individuals from other historically excluded groups in DEIB conversations, as you do not want to cause harm. Cultivating workplace environments that are safe, welcoming, inclusive, and affirming for BIPOC is an important retention strategy mentioned in the literature. This is only possible if individuals in these communities feel safe in your environment. This is important so they do not feel singled out or that you are putting undue pressure on them to speak up. Cultivating an environment where they feel safe requires a psychologically safe environment.

Achieving this type of environment is rooted in the concept of psychological safety. Edmondson (1999) describes psychological safety as a shared belief held by team members that the team is safe for interpersonal risk-taking. Risk-taking behaviors include speaking up, asking for help, admitting errors, and experimenting. Bresman and Edmondson (2022) add that psychological safety is "a shared belief that team members will not be rejected or embarrassed for speaking up with their ideas, questions, or concerns." In their article, Writer and Watson (2019) highlight the significance of establishing sanctuary spaces that allow faculty of color to connect, find affinity, and experience a sense of safety. Bresman and Edmondson (2022) surmise that psychological safety is the key to unlocking the benefits of diversity.

In my library, meaningfully and authentically engaging in conversations has yielded positive results. I have found that periodic check-in meetings with library workers who do not report directly to me help me build trust with my team members. These conversations have allowed me to learn more about what excites them about their work, what challenges or barriers they may face, and other items they feel comfortable sharing. The conversations are not fishing expeditions but rather an opportunity to engage in a two-way dialogue where I share things about myself too. It helps them to get to know me better as well. These conversations have motivated me not to make assumptions about people. I do not know their stories or what they deal with outside of work. These regular conversations make staff feel comfortable sharing positive or negative experiences or interactions during the workday.

While I may not be able to immediately act on every request an employee has, having conversations signals that I care and value their feedback, and it allows me to engage in a meaningful conversation with the employee about how they are doing, ask about barriers or boulders I can help remove, and what specific things they need to do their work. These conversations are two-way streets where

I have found that telling my story and listening to theirs helps me find common ground with my team members. Knowing what excites a staff member makes advocating for them an easier process.

Play 7—Practicing Empathy

Think back to a time when you were excluded, whether it was not being picked for a kickball team as a child, not invited to a friend's wedding, not picked for a job for which you had qualifications, or left out because of your weight, gender identity, sexual orientation, or because you did not speak the language. Now, I want you to consider some adjectives describing how you felt then. Being excluded is not limited to race or gender. You have likely experienced exclusion at some point in your life. I invite you to use DEIB as the catalyst for expanding your understanding of what it means to be excluded. In addition, expand your awareness of the definitions of oppression, marginalization, power, and privilege and how the interplay of these concepts has likely left people in your libraries standing on the sidelines. The first step is to study the role that systematic racism, oppression, white supremacy, marginalization, power, and privilege have played in libraries. Increasing your knowledge will position you to use your voice when you hear a marginalized person, or anyone, being offended, get in the game, and intercede on their behalf.

Play 8—Knowing the Law

You must become familiar with various federal and state statutes relating to DEIB. The U.S. Equal Employment Opportunity Commission (EEOC) enforces federal laws prohibiting workplace discrimination. Foundational anti-discrimination laws, of which you should learn the basics, are:

- Title VII of the Civil Rights Act of 1964
- The Pregnancy Discrimination Act of 1978 (PDA)
- The Equal Pay Act of 1963 (EPA)
- The Age Discrimination in Employment Act of 1967 (ADEA)
- Title IX of the Education Amendment of 1972
- Rehabilitation Act of 1973
- Americans with Disabilities Act of 1990 (ADA)
- Civil Rights Act of 1991
- The Family and Medical Leave Act of 1993 (FMLA)
- Genetic Information Nondiscrimination Act of 2008 (GINA)

Baldwin (2022) noted that the statutes mentioned paved the way for modern-day DEI laws, and employers now have guidance on what does (and does not) work to promote diversity, equity, and inclusion in the workplace (para 1). I recommend that as a library manager you should have a basic understanding of these laws. Your institution's human resources personnel will guide you in navigating and interpreting these laws.

There may also be state laws of which you should be aware. For example, in my home state of South Carolina, we have the South Carolina Human Affairs Law, which states:

> It is illegal to discriminate against someone (applicant or employee) because of that person's race, color, religion, sex (including pregnancy, childbirth, lactation, or related medical condition), national origin, age (40 or older), or disability. It is also illegal to retaliate against a person because he or she complained about discrimination, filed a charge of discrimination, or participated in an employment discrimination investigation or lawsuit. The law forbids discrimination in every aspect of employment. (South Carolina Human Affairs Commission 2023)

In 2018, the South Carolina legislature passed the South Carolina Pregnancy Accommodations Act, which amended the South Carolina Human Affairs law. This new law requires . . .

... employers with at least 15 employees to provide reasonable accommodations to employees for medical needs arising from pregnancy, childbirth, or other related medical conditions (including lactation) unless the employer can demonstrate that the accommodation would impose an undue hardship on the operation of the business. (Satterfield and Satterfield 2018)

Knowing the basics about these laws increases my awareness of DEIB statutes and positions me to support library workers during various life stages.

An important action for Play 8 is to build strong relationships with your Office of Equity or Diversity and Inclusion, Human Resources, the Office of the General Counsel, and the Ombudsperson. Individuals in these offices will be key allies in helping you to navigate laws and policies.

Play 9—Encouraging Continuous Learning

Lifelong learning is the focus of Play 9. Maya Angelou, the American poet and civil rights activist, said, "Do the best you can until you know better. Then do better when you know better." As a DEIB practitioner, I aim to be open to learning new concepts and approaches. I have had the opportunity to participate in various professional development opportunities that have helped me build leadership skills and move beyond my comfort zone. You should seek training and development opportunities to become a more equitable, inclusive practitioner. Here are a few examples of impactful development opportunities I have completed:

- DeEtta Jones and Associates offers an Inclusive Managers Toolkit: https://www.deettajones.com/.
- Right to Be Bystander Intervention Training: https://righttobe.org/bystander-intervention-training/.
- Racial Equity Institute: https://racialequityinstitute.org/.
- Safe Zone Project Training: https://thesafezoneproject.com/.

There are countless books about DEIB topics that can heighten your awareness of the lived experiences of people whose identities differ from yours. Reading is just one step. You can join a book discussion group such as MLA Reads, a virtual book discussion group for information professionals that centers on conversations about equity, diversity, and inclusion (Williams 2022, para 1). Since 2018, MLA Reads has endeavored to create a safe learning environment where information professionals can discuss difficult topics related to diversity, equity, and inclusion, engage other information professionals in conversations related to diversity, equity, and inclusion, provide a method for information professionals to participate no matter what type of library they work in or where they are physically located, and connect librarians with similar interests to assist with networking (Jones et al. 2022). Books that the group has read include:

- *Blindspot: Hidden Bias of Good People* by Mahzarin Banaji, PhD, and Anthony Greenwald, PhD
- *The Person You Mean to Be: How Good People Fight Bias* by Dolly Chugh, PhD
- *Black Man in a White Coat: A Doctor's Reflections on Race and Medicine* by Damon Tweedy, MD
- *Caste: The Origins of Our Discontents* by Isabel Wilkerson
- *What the Eyes Don't See: A Story of Crisis, Resistance, and Hope in an American City* by Mona Hanna-Attisha, MD, MPH, FAAP

Several documentaries and films offer first-hand accounts of people's lived experiences. My favorite places to find documentaries are Netflix, various streaming services, YouTube, and my local library. Among the most thought-provoking films that have helped me to examine my privileges and assumptions are:

- *13th* (2016), directed by Ava DuVernay
- *Hello, Privilege. It's Me, Chelsea* (2019), directed by Alex Stapleton and starring Chelsea Handler
- *Brené Brown: The Call to Courage* (2019), directed by Sandra Restrepo and starring Brené Brown

- *Crip Camp: A Disability Revolution* (2020), directed by James Lebrecht and Nicole Newnham
- *Disclosure: Trans Lives on Screen* (2020), directed by Sam Feder

These are just a few examples. When stretching yourself and learning more about people with different identities, choose pathways that address gaps in your knowledge.

Play 10—Avoiding Being Performative

The focus of Play 10 is to encourage you not to do the following when managing DEIB in your library. First, avoid being performative in your actions. Performative diversity refers to the superficial efforts made by companies to create the appearance of diversity and inclusivity without actually addressing the underlying issues of systemic bias and inequality (McDuffie 2023). Morris explains performative allyship as occurring . . .

> . . . where those with privilege profess solidarity with a cause. This assumed solidarity is usually vocalized, disingenuous, and potentially harmful to marginalized groups. Often, the performative ally professes allegiance to distance themselves from potential scrutiny. (Morris 2020)

An example of being performative I have experienced in the library environment is people who consistently attend DEIB workshops or trainings but fail to apply the information learned in their professional practice. Standing in solidarity with groups from historically excluded groups with no genuine intent to take meaningful action is a harmful and hurtful example of performative DEIB. In October 2021, the Disabled Academic Collective reminded its Twitter followers:

> Celebrating Disability Awareness Month without looking over their campus policies regarding faculty hiring, student recruitment, and retention of faculty, staff, or students [is a missed opportunity]. If you're "celebrating" our existence in #HigherEd, you should also be listening to all of the stories where we've recounted barriers, discrimination, neglect, and abuse by academic systems. See #WhyDisabledPeopleDropout. And you should be doing the real work of implementing policy changes and investing money in disability culture. If you're an educator or admin—read about academic ableism. (@DisabledAcadem 2021)

I also encourage you to stop asking BIPOC information professionals to nominate other BIPOCs for your applicant pool if your institution is not serious about giving their applications full consideration.

The point is that moving beyond being performative is about taking action. Richard-Craven (2023) offers several strategies for practicing non-performative DEI that align with the plays recommended in this chapter, including educating yourself, sharing your workplace diversity statistics, and having real conversations.

Designing the Arena

Many of our libraries are housed in older buildings that have not been renovated. For library workers to do their best work in your arena, you must consider what it feels like to work or navigate the library's physical space. To guide your explorations of your space, ask the question: Are all really welcome to use your space? To help you decide, consider the following questions:

1. Does the library worker who navigates your space in a wheelchair, a walker, crutches, or using a cane feel free to move about your space safely?
2. Will individuals who are lactating or those who need space to pray or disconnect find that they belong in your space?
3. Can a non-binary individual use a restroom where they feel safe? The strategies listed in this section will go a long way to support belonging in your environment.
4. Has the use of pronouns normalized in your environment and systems?

Are you accommodating the many individuals who use your space? Some common methods include:

- **Normalize pronouns**. The ALA suggests that libraries "normalize using the pronoun 'they' when speaking about patrons" (American Library Association 2023). Kehrein (2016) offers excellent strategies and "gender-less library phrases" to help library staff improve customer service skills using gender-neutral terms. While the article is directed toward communicating with library patrons, the message applies to communication among staff as well. Noted author Maud Newton has asserted that "y'all" is the most inclusive of all pronouns (Newton 2022). The key with pronouns is to ask individuals for their pronoun preferences or to address them by their names. Currier and White (2019) offer a guide on creating a trans-inclusive library and provide activities that libraries and institutions can complete to create a more inclusive environment for trans students, employees, and patrons.
- **Converting an existing restroom or adding all-gender restroom options**. Currier and White (2019) suggest that this is one of the easiest changes a library can make to affirm its support for the trans community. During my library's recent renovation, we added multiple all-gender restrooms to the building.
- **Providing spaces for lactating mothers**. Adcock et al. (2019) shared their experiences transforming an unused library office into a nursing mother's room at the Rowland Medical Library. The authors offered several practical steps for libraries to consider when undertaking a similar project, including, but not limited to, finding a champion, developing room policies, marketing, and housekeeping. The South Carolina Lactation Support Act was signed into law in 2020, which states that "employers must make reasonable efforts to provide a room or other location, other than a toilet stall, in close proximity to the work area where an employee may express milk in privacy" (McCoy 2020). The law clarifies that employers are not required to build a room for the primary purpose of expressing breast milk. Prior to the law being passed, several lactation rooms existed on our campus, but none were based outside the library. Fortunately, we were able to add a lactation room to our renovation plans in 2021, as it was a commonly requested need.
- **Using gender-neutral language in signage**. Delfino (2022) defined gender-neutral language as simply a way of talking about people without assuming their gender. Examples of gender-neutral words offered by Delfino include *workers, salesperson, chair, chairperson,* and *postal worker*.

Paying attention to accessibility standards for virtual and physical spaces is another inclusive practice that must be considered when managing DEIB. Regarding your virtual spaces, libraries must consider what it is like to navigate the library's website using assistive devices. Equally important is considering what it feels like to navigate the library's physical spaces. Pionke (2019) encouraged librarians to conduct accessibility walk-throughs of their spaces while considering the following questions:

1. What does this space look like for someone who is four feet tall?
2. What does this space look like for someone who does not have any hands?
3. What would this space be like for someone who cannot see it?

In 2019, I attended a workshop where participants were asked if Braille markings were available on their elevator buttons. Embarrassingly, I could not answer immediately. I assumed this was an ADA standard, but I was unsure. The reason for my uncertainty was that I do not use Braille to navigate the world. This is an excellent example of how we fail to see (no pun intended) things that do not impact us personally.

When purchasing new furniture, purchase furniture that accommodates a variety of body types. For instance, one of the things that my library has done when purchasing chairs is to have the vendor bring multiple chairs onsite to fit a variety of weight capacities and heights for staff to try out for a few weeks. This allows individuals to sit in various chairs to make evidence-based decisions according to their height and weight. A key aspect of our recent renovation was allowing students and library workers to try out some of the new furniture we were considering before the final purchase was made.

Factor in diverse dietary needs when planning parties. When planning parties or other gatherings, it is important to remember that not everyone drinks alcoholic or sugar-laden beverages. Ensure that non-alcoholic drinks, water, and sugar-free options are available. Again, asking people what they need to enjoy the event will be helpful.

Conclusion

This chapter discussed insights learned from managing DEIB in an academic health sciences library. The chapter focused exclusively on managing DEIB for library staff. The chapter emphasizes the role of library leadership in ensuring DEIB is incorporated into library environments and offers suggestions on how to accomplish this. Using the arena analogy, the author described the mindset needed for leaders to successfully adopt DEIB in their libraries. Much of this mindset is influenced by the leader's identity and how they use their privilege in the arena for the greater good of the library program. Like an athletic coach, the library leader must enter the DEIB arena prepared to guide their team.

In the second half of the chapter, the author shared ten strategies from her DEIB playbook. Among the plays highlighted were practicing self-reflection, assessing the library's current DEIB reality, recruiting and retaining players, asking people what they need to be successful, inviting a diverse group of people to the decision-making table, engaging in critical conversations thoughtfully and authentically, practicing empathy, knowing the law, encouraging continuous learning, and avoiding being performative. In all, managing DEIB in libraries is no small task. The DEIB journey requires the leader to enter the arena fully committed to the work, armed with a plan, and prepared to take intentional action toward making their environment as welcoming, safe, inclusive, and affirming as possible for all its players.

Discussion Questions

1. When people finish their tenure working for your library, what do you want them to look like psychologically, emotionally, and physiologically?
2. What makes your library a good place to work?
3. What are you hoping to enable by employing a diverse workforce?

Works Cited

Adcock, Sarah, Elizabeth Hinton, Susan Clark, and Chameka Robinson. 2019. "Supporting Breastfeeding Mothers by Transforming Library Space: A Nursing Mothers Room Project." *Journal of Hospital Librarianship* 19, no. 3: 201–13. Accessed July 8, 2023. https://doi.org/10.1080/15323269.2019.1628559.

American Association of University Women (AAUW). n.d. "Diversity Equity & Inclusion Toolkit. Getting Started with Difficult Conversations." Accessed May 8, 2023. https://www.aauw.org/resources/member/governance-tools/dei-toolkit/difficult-conversations/.

American Library Association. Allied Professional Association. 2014. "Pay equity." Accessed July 6, 2023. https://ala-apa.org/improving-salariesstatus/pay-equity/.

American Library Association. 2017. "Member Demographics Study." Accessed July 7, 2023. https://www.ala.org/tools/research/initiatives/membershipsurveys.

———. 2023. "Libraries Respond: Protecting and Supporting Transgender Staff and Patrons." Accessed July 9, 2023. https://www.ala.org/advocacy/diversity/librariesrespond/transgender-staff-patrons.

American Psychological Association. 2023. *APA Dictionary of Psychology*. Accessed May 6, 2023. https://dictionary.apa.org/.

Baldwin, Kelsi. August 12, 2022. "Federal Laws Protecting Diversity in the Workplace." *Mississippi College Law Review*. Accessed July 2, 2023. https://mclawreview.org/2022/08/12/federal-laws-protecting-diversity-in-the-workplace/.

Banaji, Mahzarin R., and Anthony G. Greenwald. 2016. *Blindspot: The Hidden Biases of Good People.* New York: Random House Publishing Group.

Bresman, Henrik, and Amy C. Edmondson. March 17, 2022. "Research: To Excel, Diverse Teams Need Psychological Safety." *Harvard Business Review.* Accessed July 2, 2023. https://hbr.org/2022/03/research-to-excel-diverse-teams-need-psychological-safety.

Bright, Kawanna, and Joanna Nelson Rendón. May 14, 2021. "Slicing into the Privilege Layer Cake." *Intersections, A Blog on Diversity, Literacy, and Outreach.* Accessed July 5, 2023. https://www.ala.org/advocacy/diversity/odlos-blog/slicing-privilege-layer-cake.

"Conversation Ground Rules (Infographic)." October 16, 2016. *Catalyst.* Accessed July 2, 2023. https://www.catalyst.org/research/conversation-ground-rules/.

Chugh, Dolly. 2018a. *The Person You Mean to Be: How Good People Fight Bias.* New York: Harper Business.

———. September 18, 2018b. "Use Your Everyday Privilege to Help Others." *Harvard Business Review.* Accessed July 2, 2023. https://hbr.org/2018/09/use-your-everyday-privilege-to-help-others.

Currier, Brett D., and Tessa White. September 30, 2019. "Creating the Trans Inclusive Library." Assessed July 8, 2023. https://doi.org/10.31229/osf.io/re8gf.

Delfino, Devon. 2022. "How to Use Gender-Neutral Language at Work and in Life." *Grammarly.* Accessed July 6, 2023. https://www.grammarly.com/blog/gender-neutral-language/.

Dictionary.com. 2023. "Echo Chamber Definition & Meaning." Accessed July 6, 2023. https://www.dictionary.com/browse/echo-chamber.

Disabled Academic Collective. 2021. "Performative Allyship is Not Activism." Twitter. Accessed July 2, 2023. https://twitter.com/DisabledAcadem/status/1445030232013123589.

Edmondson, Amy. 1999. "Psychological Safety and Learning Behavior in Work Teams." *Administrative Science Quarterly* 44, no. 2: 350–83. https://doi.org/10.2307/2666999.

Ettarh, Fobazi. January 10, 2018. "Vocational Awe and Librarianship: The Lies We Tell Ourselves." *In the Library with the Lead Pipe.* Accessed July 7, 2023. https://www.inthelibrarywiththeleadpipe.org/2018/vocational-awe/.

Finnegan, Richard P. 2018. "How to Conduct Stay Interviews: Core Features and Advantages, Part 1." Accessed May 3, 2023. https://www.shrm.org/resourcesandtools/hr-topics/employee-relations/pages/stay-interview-how-to.aspx.

GLSEN. 2023. "Guidelines for Respectful GSA Spaces." Accessed May 8, 2023. https://www.glsen.org/activity/guidelines-respectful-gsa-spaces.

Harvard Implicit Association Test (IAT). 2011. "Project Implicit." Accessed July 2, 2023. https://implicit.harvard.edu/implicit/takeatest.html.

Institute for Women's Policy Research. March 2023. "Women Earn Less than Men Whether They Work in the Same or in Different Occupations." Fact Sheet IWPR # C514. Accessed July 1, 2023. https://iwpr.org/wp-content/uploads/2023/03/Gender-Wage-Gaps-2023-003.pdf.

Jones, Shannon, Kelsa Bartley, Melissa De Santis, Ryan Harris, Don Jason, and Dede Rios. 2022. "Braving our Blind Spots: Using a Virtual Book Discussion Group to Continue Conversations on Implicit Bias in Libraries." In Corliss Lee, Brian Lym, Tatiana Bryant, Jonathan Cain, and Kenneth Schlesinger, eds. *Implementing Excellence in Diversity, Equity, and Inclusion: A Handbook for Academic Libraries*, pp. 231–55. Chicago, IL: Association of College and Research Libraries.

Kehrein, Micah. 2016. "Improve Your Customer Service Skills: Go Gender Neutral!" *Intersections.* American Library Association. Accessed July 2, 2023. https://www.ala.org/advocacy/diversity/odlos-blog/intersections-improve-your-customer-service-skills-go-gender-neutral.

Liu, Jennifer. November 30, 2021. "Why the 'Stay Interview' is the Next Big Trend of the Great Resignation." *CNBC Make It*. Accessed May 3, 2023. https://www.cnbc.com/2021/11/30/why-stay-interviews-are-the-next-big-trend-of-the-great-resignation.html.

Marin Health and Human Services. 2021. "Equity vs. Equality: What's the Difference?" Accessed July 2, 2023. https://www.marinhhs.org/sites/default/files/boards/general/equality_v._equity_04_05_2021.pdf.

McCoy, Ellison F. July 1, 2020. "South Carolina Enacts Lactation Support Act." West Harrison, NY: Jackson Lewis, PC. Accessed July 6, 2023. https://www.jacksonlewis.com/insights/south-carolina-enacts-lactation-support-act.

McDuffie, Alaina. February 28, 2023. "Avoiding the Perils of Performative Diversity." *Platform Magazine*. Accessed July 2, 2023. https://platformmagazine.org/2023/02/28/avoiding-the-perils-of-performative-diversity/.

McIntosh, Peggy. July–August 1989. "White Privilege: Unpacking the Invisible Knapsack." *Peace and Freedom Magazine*: 10–12. Women's International League for Peace and Freedom, Philadelphia, PA. Reprinted in *Privilege, Fraudulence, and Teaching as Learning*. New York: Routledge, 2019, pp. 29–34.

Medical Library Association (MLA). n.d. "Diversity, Equity, and Inclusion: Making MLA a More Diverse and Inclusive Association." Accessed April 30, 2023. https://www.mlanet.org/page/diversity-and-inclusion-team.

Morris, Carmen. November 26, 2020. "Performative Allyship: What are the Signs and Why Leaders get Exposed." *Forbes*. Accessed July 2, 2023. https://www.forbes.com/sites/carmenmorris/2020/11/26/performative-allyship-what-are-the-signs-and-why-leaders-get-exposed/?sh=609830dd22ec.

National Association of School Psychologists (NASP). 2016. "Understanding Race and Privilege." Accessed May 7, 2023. https://www.nasponline.org/resources-and-publications/resources-and-podcasts/diversity-and-social-justice/social-justice/understanding-race-and-privilege.

Newton, Maud. October 18, 2022. "Y'all: The Most Inclusive of All Pronouns." *The New York Times Magazine*. Accessed July 1, 2023. https://www.nytimes.com/2022/10/18/magazine/yall.html.

Ng, Gorick. July 21, 2021. "How to Use Your Privilege to Even the Playing Field." *Harvard Business Review: Ascend*. Accessed July 2, 2023. https://hbr.org/2021/07/how-to-use-your-privilege-to-even-the-playing-field.

Perry, Tyler. 2019. "Tyler Perry Gives Powerful Speech of Motivation as He Accepts Ultimate Icon Award. BET Awards 2019." Accessed July 6, 2023. https://www.youtube.com/watch?v=DVjjSxpqbOo.

Phillips, Katherine W. 2014. "How Diversity Makes Us Smarter." Accessed July 1, 2023. https://www.scientificamerican.com/article/how-diversity-makes-us-smarter/.

Pionke, J. J. April 8, 2019. "Librarian JJ Pionke on Diversity, Equity, and Inclusion in Libraries: 'It's Personal to Me.'" American Library Association. Accessed July 1, 2023. https://www.youtube.com/watch?v=58FmnzlFzzs&t=46s.

Richard-Craven, Maya. 2023. "Here's How to Practice Non-Performative DEI." *Forbes*. Accessed July 2, 2023. https://www.forbes.com/sites/mayarichard-craven/2023/04/20/heres-how-to-practice-non-performative-dei/.

Roosevelt, Theodore. n.d. "The Man in the Arena." The Theodore Roosevelt Center at Dickinson State University, Dickinson, ND. Accessed May 5, 2023. https://www.theodorerooseveltcenter.org/Learn-About-TR/TR-Encyclopedia/Culture-and-Society/Man-in-the-Arena.aspx.

Satterfield, Stephanie E., and Andreas N. Satterfield. 2018. "South Carolina Enacts New Pregnancy Accommodation Requirements." West Harrison, NY: JacksonLewis, PC. Accessed May 7, 2023. https://www.jacksonlewis.com/publication/south-carolina-enacts-new-pregnancy-accommodation-requirements.

Society of Human Resource Management (SHRM). 2023. "What is Meant by 'Belonging' in the Workplace, and How Can It be Measured?" Accessed July 2, 2023. https://www.shrm.org/resourcesandtools/tools-and-samples/hr-qa/pages/belonging-in-the-workplace.aspx.

South Carolina Human Affairs Commission. 2023. "South Carolina Human Affairs Law. Prohibited Practices & Discrimination Types." Accessed May 7, 2023. https://schac.sc.gov/employment-discrimination/prohibited-practices-discrimination-types.

Spar, Benjamin, Colleen Dye, Rachel Lefkowitz, and Deanna Pate. 2018. "2018 Workplace Learning Report: The Rise and Responsibility of Talent Development in the New Labor Market." *LinkedIn Learning*. http://hdl.voced.edu.au/10707/451861.

U.S. Bureau of Labor Statistics. 2022. "Labor Force Statistics from the Current Population Survey 2022." January 25, 2023. Accessed July 5, 2023. https://www.bls.gov/cps/cpsaat11.htm.

U.S. Equal Employment Opportunity Commission. n.d. "Laws Enforced by EEOC." Accessed May 7, 2023. https://www.eeoc.gov/statutes/laws-enforced-eeoc.

Vinopal, Jennifer. 2016. "The Quest for Diversity in Library Staffing: From Awareness to Action." *In the Library with the Lead Pipe*. Accessed July 2, 2023. http://www.inthelibrarywiththeleadpipe.org/2016/quest-for-diversity/.

Williams, Jamia. 2022. "What Is MLA Reads? Interview with Shannon Jones." *Infobase*. Accessed May 7, 2023. https://infobase.com/blog/what-is-mla-reads-interview-with-shannon-jones/.

Writer, Jeanette Haynes, and Dwight C. Watson. 2019. "Recruitment and Retention: An Institutional Imperative Told through the Storied Lenses of Faculty of Color." *Journal of the Professoriate* 10, no. 2: 23–46.

4

Staff Support—Leading and Valuing All Library Employees

Katie Prentice

Key Points

Library staff support is an idea. It is a concept that should be on the minds of library leaders. Without library staff, our libraries would be warehouses of stuff, rather than dynamic service-oriented organizations supporting education, research, and clinical care. This idea of staff support should then be well-defined in library science literature, and yet a search for "staff support" in *Library, Information Science & Technology Abstracts* (LISTA) in late 2022 finds only sixty-eight results. Consulting the LISTA thesaurus identifies a potentially better term in *LIBRARY personnel management* (offering only 252 results), but the term does not include a formal definition. This chapter will discuss leading and valuing all library employees, including the hiring, retention, and management of staff. By attempting to find new meaning and focus for library leaders and employees at all levels, this chapter will share ideas and resources to further develop and enhance the concept of staff support.

Finding Meaning

The terms used in this chapter will encompass the spectrum of roles in health science libraries. Library employees, staff, and workers (at all levels) include all staff, volunteers, and students, including degreed librarians and technical or support staff. When discussing master's level professional librarians, librarian will be used. Leadership roles will be discussed as specifically as possible, and with many possible titles for director, the term director will be used to include deans and university librarians. Manager will be used for all types of managers or supervisors.

In my career, the concept of staff support (beyond my personal relations with supervisors) jumped into my everyday awareness while I was attending the Harvard Graduate School of Education professional education program *Leadership Institute for Academic Librarians* with an extensive curriculum in leadership. Toward the end of the course, the facilitated conversation shifted toward the challenges of working and leading in toxic and challenging environments. My "wow" moment was when the facilitator asked for a show of hands for everyone who was working in, or had ever worked in, a challenging environment. Nearly every hand was in the air. That moment stays with me and regularly reinforces the critical need for library leaders and managers to value and support all library employees.

The later phases of the COVID-19 pandemic, with inflation in the United States stubbornly high and generally low unemployment, has led to extensive handwringing in media outlets about "quiet quitting." The *Washington Post* defines quiet quitting "as 'working to rule' or otherwise declining to go above and beyond what you are paid to do in your job." Other sources consider it a viral term that spans both "mentally checking out" *and* "establishing healthy work-life boundaries." Putting aside the recent viral trends, the idea does not feel new, but after the waves of pandemic-related furloughs and hiring, morale may be a larger challenge than many administrators and managers appreciate. Articles on quiet quitting focus on the impact to the organization, not the employee who has set, or reinforced, boundaries with their time and energy. If an employee is not completing their work, that is a management issue. If there is too much work for one person to appropriately complete within a standard workweek, that is also a management issue that should be addressed using official policy and procedure from an established employee handbook. Communication is critical when major changes to employee productivity are detected or reported to avoid assumptions about the employee's circumstances or a manager's belief that staff overachievers are the standard situation.

The State of Library Employees

Before considering libraries, it is important to recognize the generational and cultural shifts happening in every workplace. The *2022 EY US Generation Survey* (Ernst & Young LLC 2022) finds that "92% of workers surveyed said company culture has an impact on their intent to stay with their current employer." In addition, EY reports that competitive pay and benefits are the top two factors in the decision to apply for a new position, followed by hybrid work options. Interestingly, the survey found that generational desires for flexibility are fairly consistent: 33 percent of baby boomers rated flexibility as a top factor, 35 percent of millennials cited wanting hybrid work as the reason to change jobs, 29 percent of millennials cited work-life balance, and 31 percent of Gen Z also cited flexibility in work as the most meaningful benefit. While library workers may generally have different working conditions from the workers at large organizations surveyed by EY, they are likely considering the same factors in decisions to stay with or leave a workplace.

The seminal 2017 paper by Kendrick about low morale describes the associated factors among academic librarians. Kendrick concludes that "unexpected negative event[s]" and the ensuing impacts lead to low morale along with the emotional and physical responses to the event. Adding to the complexity, the factors contributing to morale may not always be from within the library. Weyant et al. (2021a) identify a framework leading to low morale as both within the library (e.g., relationships with supervisor and other employees) as well as outside of the library (e.g., technology, economy/budgets, and society/culture). This framework is designed to show supervisors and managers clear elements to examine culture and ways to improve.

Research into organizational culture and management of libraries finds that morale "depended more on organizational factors such as the ability to progress, workload, respect, and funding" than on other issues (Glusker, 176). Communication and transparency at all levels also include awareness of current events, for example, during the early days of the COVID-19 pandemic when "supportive bosses" helped with caregiving issues and remote work while "toxic" ones expected business to continue as usual. Additionally, in 2020 Jason Martin published a study on job satisfaction, conducted the prior year, with participants recruited from ALA litervs. The study linked library job satisfaction to culture and environment, colleagues, leadership, pay, diversity and inclusion, workload, meaningful work, external recognition, external recognition of the library, and being personally valued. The trends identified in recent surveys are clear: communication, environment, and organizational functions are critical to satisfaction and morale.

What Is a Manager to Do?

While the impacts of demoralization are not easily resolved, Kendrick offers hope because the "academic librarians who have dealt with low morale are more likely to recognize and appreciate functional work environments and strive to return to one as soon as possible" (Kendrick, 2017, 874). This hope is also seen in Weyant et al. (2021a), who report that "consistent and clear communication" top-down and across the organization is key to improving morale. Cross-training and training also improve confidence and trust and shares work burdens. Even the simple act of scheduling and holding regular meetings between supervisors and employees may increase morale. Glusker et al. (2022) conclude that respectful peer collaboration should be a stated organizational value that includes staff voices at all levels in decision-making. In addition, fair pay and job security must also be considered, including allowing all staff reasonable schedule accommodations and flexibility.

True improvement in morale and job satisfaction also requires honesty and reflection about librarianship and the profession. Vocational awe, as described by Ettarh (2018), is "the set of ideas, values, and assumptions that librarians have about themselves and the profession that result in notions that libraries as institutions are inherently good, sacred notions, and therefore beyond critique." She argues that vocational awe directly correlates with burnout and low salary, giving language to the pressures of librarianship and a possible framework for healthier workplaces not directly tied to "struggle, sacrifice, and obedience" where consideration is given to both the populations served and those who work there. Managers and leaders must recognize the language and long tradition of vocational awe, to ask questions, listen to all staff, and take action against job creep, under-compensation, and low wages. While some middle managers may not have the power to effect major organizational changes, advocacy for their teams and colleagues is still important. Directors should communicate with administrators about the role, value, and impact of library staff in the greater organization as they work toward improvements in compensation as well as appropriate staffing levels.

Hiring and Transitions

According to the Bureau of Labor Statistics, the job outlook for librarians and library media specialists is positive, with expected growth in the decade from 2021 to 2031 and a stated need of "14,900 openings for librarians" as retirements and job changes happen. The job postings within health sciences libraries seem to reflect this growth trend, but changes to the library work environment, including needing fewer staff to manage smaller collections, and budget challenges have not always led to one-to-one position replacements or re-hires. New library roles are also being developed in visualization and research data management, and revisions to the *Medical Library Association Competencies for Lifelong Learning and Professional Success, 2017* reflect continued growth in the professional realm. All in all, the job market is changing, and while substantial growth in number of roles/positions may be elusive, medical school expansion plans and new schools in development may lead to the eventual creation of additional positions for health sciences librarians.

In the deep end of the metaphorical hiring pool, challenges abound. Job seekers report that they want to see transparent salary and benefit information, and yet many organizations still do not share salary ranges, or even minimum salary, in job postings. As of the end of 2022, California, Colorado, Rhode Island, Washington state, and, recently, New York City passed varied pay transparency legislation with requirements to include pay information in job posts. According to Ask A Manager's Alison Green (2022), the current lack of salary transparency is "particularly out of touch in this job market," and yet the lack of salary transparency has been covered extensively by Green for more than a decade. This issue of transparency places some health sciences workplaces in an awkward position where managers and directors may want to post salary ranges within postings but may not be permitted to do so by human resources departments or other policies. Even in such circumstances, library managers should advocate for more transparent postings that allow applicants to make their own choice to apply or not. In support of salary transparency, the Medical Library Association (MLA) online job board requires "a minimum salary; a salary range is preferred" for the postings to be approved. Individual librarians should also advocate that their other professional organizations adopt guidelines, like MLA did, that establish salary transparency as a requirement and norm of the profession.

During natural staffing transitions, as people depart from our organizations, or are promoted into new positions, it is important to remember those who are still working in their same roles. Beyond general employee retention or succession planning or organizational knowledge management, the librarians and paraprofessionals/technicians/other staff who continue to work must be supported during the departure, transition, and hiring processes. When a vacancy occurs, it is natural to want to continue every service, without change or interruption, but staff departures provide opportunity to communicate about workload and prioritize and find tasks or projects to pause or discontinue. If a staff person is taking on critical or extra duties during a vacancy, in addition to their regular tasks, check with human resources to see if additional temporary compensation can be arranged. This may not be possible in every organization, but one-time funds (or bonuses) could assist with the recognition for the person(s) taking on extra work.

Additionally, this is the time for directors to find the courage to say no to new commitments for the library organization and support staff who express concern about workload. In 2009, Ford determined that 'the ability to say no . . . is directly related to mental wellness and a health work/life balance" so library leaders must be aware of workload challenges and respond to staff needs. It is striking that Ford describes saying no as taking "a tremendous amount of emotional intelligence, leadership, and, let's face it, guts" because accepting no from staff requires the same things. While library leaders will need to ensure that the organization's work is completed, they must also have staff to effectively do the work. I learned to use the improvisational comedy technique of "yes, and . . ." with a suggestion or alternate plan to avoid a direct no and a defensive response. I share this with colleagues and staff to open communication and look for a path forward because it usually results in a conversation and mutual agreement on a reasonable plan.

Retention

Once staff have been hired and get past the first few days, a sigh of relief likely emanates from the director's office. From the moment a new employee begins to the moment they decide to leave could be days to years. I remember starting my first health sciences library job with the idea in my head to stay around three years and to use that time to figure out where I wanted to be next. It never dawned on me on day one that I would be there for nearly nine years before departing to shift into a higher-level managerial role. It is likely that most staff want to stay, want to feel supported, and do not want to go through the trouble of the job search and potential move. When morale issues resolve and job satisfaction is present, academic librarians "feel significant levels of relief and renewal of interest in their work." Weyant et al. (2021b) found that "supportive mentoring can help professionals grow into librarians who are more effective" and confident. Identifying, joining, and supporting the programs and connections around career growth is critical to staff support because action (and funding, if needed) connects to the value of staff.

In an ideal world, every library would have adequate support for wages, professional development, and professional association activity. Both training and continuing education have been linked to increasing morale, so directors must develop and implement plans for equitable distribution of funding and resources, including time for learning opportunities. On an individual level, Miller Waltz (2021) suggests that "learning is an ultimate act of hope," and learning is a good way to be open to new and different opportunities. While the pandemic disrupted many conferences and trainings and shifted many events online and to hybrid format, continued conversations about whether employees want to travel should be considered.

The concept of flourishing was explored by Miller Waltz in the context of engaging and motivating colleagues. Miller Waltz suggests that shifting "discussions to focus on engagement and flourishing, rather than burnout" can move our professional conversations in a better direction. She argues that the issues of burnout and low morale were not new to the COVID-19 pandemic and existed long before by citing a 1983 article on burnout. Suggested practices to support colleagues include engagement through initiative since "relationships and connections play in how we feel about work." Miller Waltz also explores theories of motivation as a critical need because motivated people feel "confident, satisfied, empowered, and cared for" and that is a recipe for an employee staying in their job. Importantly, Miller Waltz calls attention to the importance of self-care through sustainable and healthy coping practices. The 2022 development of the Be Well MLA initiative, designed to promote "wellness and well-being among members of the Medical Library Association," is an excellent source of content and inspiration to explore wellness for librarians (Jones 2022). Managers can work towards connections at the workplace and even encourage exploration of wellness for all staff. At the same time, all staff should keep in mind their own wellness and boundaries and act accordingly.

Honesty and Challenging Conversations

Supporting staff spans everything from celebrating wins to addressing concerns and conflicts. Hiring is the start of a new role, and the decision to leave and finally depart is the end. Retaining the right employees requires self-awareness regarding conflict and awareness of the factors that lead to an employee's decision to depart. Conflict avoidance "attempts to avoid directly confronting the issue," often by changing the subject or never bringing up or allowing discussion on the topic. Recognizing and addressing conflict or other workplace challenges is a choice. It is rarely comfortable, but an honest approach is the best method. Similarly, truly supporting individuals for their decisions to stay or move from an organization is also a choice. In smaller libraries with fewer opportunities to move up or supervise, changing jobs is often the only way for some librarians to gain additional experience in management. Leaving for growth is not a personal slight to a director or manager; it is a personal decision made in the best interest of the individual and should be supported even when the departure of a valued staff person will create a challenge for the library.

The book *Radical Candor* by Kim Scott (2019) encourages direct communication that includes both kind and clear criticism and specific *and* sincere praise. Radical candor is based on the philosophy of "Caring Personally while Challenging Directly" to avoid small issues becoming large issues, or even the worst-case scenario of the departure of valued staff. Using the philosophy of radical candor to negate conflict avoidance is a solid beginning to supporting staff with transparency and honesty. Similarly, the Potential Project (2022) published insights showing that "care for employees within and beyond the boundaries of office walls and candor to deliver important messages with honesty," with the caveat that candor is "not brutal honesty," is highly effective and desired by employees. The takeaway for all levels of employees is to embrace care and candor and look for ways to improve organizational transparency. This is not to say that everything should be shared. Confidentiality, when needed, is also important for managers to observe out of respect for staff.

Additional research provides insight into the reasons library staff choose to leave. Kendrick (2021) identified factors including anger, career expectations, mobility, equity, diversity and inclusion, organizational culture, and workplace expectations as reasons for deciding to leave and corresponding limitations to departure, including family, economic, and geographical concerns. She further notes that when someone begins at a new position after leaving another, both uncertainty and mistrust continue for the employee and often manifest with anticipated fear or guarded behavior. The conclusion Kendrick draws compels leaders to be present and transparent as well as empathetic when workplace challenges are observed or reported. Kendrick also prompts leaders and managers to review hiring processes (such as calling prior supervisors) and to apply trauma-informed leadership to assist employees in the workplace. Even library leaders and managers that are part of much larger organizations can learn more about why staff leave and look for ways to improve the complete work experience.

Support in Action

The realm of research into work often feels abstract, so how does leading and valuing employees work? I wish it was simple, but the process does not have an endpoint. Research from Potential

Project's The Human Leader study on what employees want in a good boss reveals that employees want leaders to be good at the job and be good human beings (Hougaard 2022). The traits that were identified included being competent, capable, and balanced as well as trustworthy, sincere, and considerate. The key to this research is that "competence and compassion are not an either/or state," and library leaders can take this to heart and work toward a balance between performance and personal development. Workshops, conferences, and opportunities to learn and develop skills will allow both new and experienced leaders to continue their leadership growth. The recently developed Conference on Academic Library Management (CALM) is a great example of a conference focused on practical management skills for "middle managers, administrators, coordinators, and those that aspire" to more effective management. I have found the CALM sessions to be remarkable opportunities to learn and reflect on many aspects of management.

Final Thoughts

This chapter presented a look at staff support to assist current and future library directors in improvement as employers and managers by integrating different (or new) operational practices and concepts. None of us is perfect, and mistakes will be made. By being honest, we can improve the cultures of our organizations and find better paths forward. Honest conversations about burnout, morale, workload, activities, equity and inclusion, and priorities will support the process. When an employee is truly not completing their duties, follow internal procedures with human resources (and/or staff handbook) because to do nothing will create additional challenges for other staff, as well as the constituent groups served by the library, leading to resentment and frustration and additional low morale.

By recognizing and honoring the whole and unique people working with me, I can bring myself to conversations and find balance among my needs, employee needs, and the needs of my library. Since becoming a manager years ago, I have considered supervision an exercise of Venn diagrams. Personally, I am one circle, the organization is one circle, and the employee is the third circle. Each part of the diagram has needs, wants, dreams, interests, and priorities, and yet we overlap in the center. I believe this perspective gives me the balance to listen, communicate, and act appropriately. More concretely, the perspective allows me to ask a new employee how they want to be supervised, or even what kind (and when) they prefer meetings to occur, in addition to communicating what I need to happen. Keeping in mind deeply entrenched vocational awe and not idealizing the profession is also part of this process.

If you are reading this chapter and feel both empowered and exhausted, you are not alone. I also hope you have a glimmer of hope for current and future leaders to work more actively to support staff and develop healthy and thoughtful organizations. These changes will not happen overnight, but each new supervisor determined to act with empathy and compassion and a "zero-tolerance outlook on workplace abuse" can begin to make a difference. Both future research and professional development have the potential to provide employees and managers with much-needed skills and opportunities.

Discussion Questions

1. What is one thing you can do to better communicate your needs to your manager or supervisor?
2. What changes can be implemented in your library to provide better support for all employees?
3. What can new library managers do to break the cycles of dysfunction? (What will you do differently when you manage or supervise?)

Recommended Reading

Brown, Brené. 2018. *Dare to Lead: Brave Work. Tough Conversations. Whole Hearts.* New York: Random House.
Green, Alison. *Ask A Manager.* https://www.askamanager.org/.

Green, Alison. 2018. *Ask a Manager: How to Navigate Clueless Colleagues, Lunch-Stealing Bosses, and the Rest of Your Life at Work.* New York: Ballantine Books.

Jones, Shannon D., and Beverly Murphy. 2019. *Diversity and Inclusion in Libraries: A Call to Action and Strategies for Success.* Lanham, MD: Rowman & Littlefield.

Scott, Kim. 2022. *Radical Candor: How to Get What You Want by Saying What You Mean.* London, England: Pan Books.

Works Cited

Bureau of Labor Statistics. 2022. "Librarians and Library Media Specialists." *Occupational Outlook Handbook*, October 4, 2022. https://www.bls.gov/ooh/education-training-and-library/librarians.htm.

"Conference on Academic Library Management (CALM)." *Conference on Academic Library Management*. Accessed November 22, 2022. https://www.conferenceonacademiclibrarymanagement.com.

"Conflict Avoidance." *Wikipedia*, March 24, 2022. https://en.wikipedia.org/wiki/Conflict_avoidance.

EBSCO Information Services, Inc. 2022. "Library, Information Science and Technology Abstracts." *EBSCO Information Services, Inc.* Accessed November 1, 2022, https://www.ebsco.com/products/research-databases/library-information-science-and-technology-abstracts.

Ernst & Young LLP (EY US). 2022. "The 2022 EY US Generation Survey," *The 2022 EY US Generation Survey: Addressing Diverse Workplace Preferences.* Accessed November 22, 2022, https://www.ey.com/en_us/diversity-inclusiveness/the-2022-ey-us-generation-survey.

Ettarh, Fobazi. 2018. "Vocational Awe and Librarianship: The Lies We Tell Ourselves." *In the Library with the Lead Pipe*, January 10, 2018. https://www.inthelibrarywiththeleadpipe.org/2018/vocational-awe/.

Ford, Emily. 2009. "How Do You Say No?" *In the Library with the Lead Pipe*, December 16, 2009. https://www.inthelibrarywiththeleadpipe.org/2009/how-do-you-say-no/.

Glusker, Ann, et al. 2022. "'Viewed as Equals': The Impacts of Library Organizational Cultures and Management on Library Staff Morale." *Journal of Library Administration* 62, no. 2 (February 17, 2022): 153–89, doi:10.1080/01930826.2022.2026119.

Green, Alison. 2022. "Why Don't Recruiters Send Me Any Information on the Jobs They're Recruiting Me For?" *Ask a Manager*, June 6, 2022. https://www.askamanager.org/2022/06/why-dont-recruiters-send-me-any-information-on-the-jobs-theyre-recruiting-me-for.html.

———. 2013. "Why Employers Won't Name a Salary Range First." *Ask a Manager*, September 30. https://www.askamanager.org/2013/09/why-employers-wont-name-a-salary-range-first.html.

Harvard Graduate School of Education. n.d. "Leadership Institute for Academic Librarians." *Harvard Graduate School of Education*, accessed November 2, 2022. https://www.gse.harvard.edu/ppe/program/leadership-institute-academic-librarians.

Hougaard, Rasmus. 2022. "Direct Leaders Are Faster, Smarter and Better." *Potential Project*, September 2022. https://www.potentialproject.com/insights/why-being-a-direct-leader-is-faster-smarter-and-better-forbes.

Jones, Shannon D. 2022. "Blogs: Be Well MLA Wednesdays: I Wet My Plants: Plants and Gardening for Wellness." *MLA Connect*, September 8, 2022. https://www.mlanet.org/p/bl/et/blogid=140&blogaid=4113.

Kendrick, Kaetrena Davis. 2017. "The Low Morale Experience of Academic Librarians: A Phenomenological Study." *Journal of Library Administration* 57, no. 8 (November 17, 2017): 846–78, doi:10.1080/01930826.2017.1368325.

———. 2021. "Leaving the Low-Morale Experience: A Qualitative Study." *ALKI: The Washington Library Association Journal* 37, no. 2 (July 2021): 9–24. https://www.wla.org/alki-home.

Liaison Committee on Medical Education: AAMC. n.d. "Regional Campus Expansion Plans at Medical School Programs." *AAMC*. Accessed December 21, 2022. https://www.aamc.org/data-reports/curriculum-reports/interactive-data/regional-campus-expansion-plans-medical-school-programs.

Lemmer, Mary. 2017. "Saying 'Yes, and' — A Principle for Improv, Business & Life." May 24, 2017. https://medium.com/improv4/saying-yes-and-a-principle-for-improv-business-life-fd050bccf7e3.

Martin, Jason. 2020. "Job Satisfaction of Professional Librarians and Library Staff." *Journal of Library Administration* 60, no. 4 (May 18, 2020): 365–82, doi:10.1080/01930826.2020.1721941.

Medical Library Association. 2017. "MLA Competencies for Lifelong Learning and Professional Success, 2017." *MEDLIIB-ED*, 2017. http://www.medlib-ed.org/competencies.

Medical Library Association. 2022. "Submitting a Job Ad." *MLA: Medical Library Association*. Accessed November 22, 2022. https://www.mlanet.org/p/cm/ld/fid=233.

Miller, Karla L. 2022. "After 'Quiet Quitting,' Here Comes 'Quiet Firing.'" *The Washington Post*, September 2, 2022, online edition. https://www.washingtonpost.com/business/2022/09/01/quiet-quitting-and-firing/.

Miller Waltz, Rebecca. 2021. "In Support of Flourishing: Practices to Engage, Motivate, Affirm, and Appreciate." *International Information & Library Review* 53, no. 4 (October 2, 2021): 333–40, doi:10.1080/10572317.2021.1990564.

Ofgang, Erik. 2022. "Quiet Quitting in Education." *Tech & Learning*, September 2022. https://issuu.com/futurepublishing/docs/tle25.digital_sept_2022?fr=sYmIwMDUxNzU0MzE.

Potential Project: The Human Leader. 2022. "It's Time to Eliminate Bad Bosses. They Are Harmful and Expensive." Spring 2022. https://global-uploads.webflow.com/5ff86e096165bce79acc825c/626a9680bd2492ee5380b145_THL%20Fourth%20Edition.pdf.

"Salary Transparency Laws Aim to Combat Pay Disparities," *US News & World Report*, October 31, 2022. Accessed November 10, 2022. https://www.usnews.com/news/us/articles/2022-10-31/salary-transparency-laws-aim-to-combat-pay-disparities.

Scott, Kim. 2019. *Radical Candor: How to Get What You Want by Saying What You Mean* (London, England: Pan Books).

U.S. Bureau of Labor Statistics. "Consumer Prices up 7.7 Percent over Year Ended October 2022: The Economics Daily." November 17, 2022. https://www.bls.gov/opub/ted/2022/consumer-prices-up-7-7-percent-over-year-ended-october-2022.htm.

"Venn Diagram." *Wikipedia*, November 17, 2022. https://en.wikipedia.org/wiki/Venn_diagram.

Weyant, Emily C., Rick L. Wallace, and Nakia J. Woodward. 2021a. "Contributions to Low Morale, Part 1: Review of Existing Literature on Librarian and Library Staff Morale." *Journal of Library Administration* 61, no. 7 (October 3, 2021): 854–68, doi:10.1080/01930826.2021.1972732.

———. 2021b. "Suggestions for Improving Morale, Part 2: Review of Existing Literature on Librarian and Library Staff Morale." *Journal of Library Administration* 61, no. 8 (November 17, 2021): 996–1007, doi:10.1080/01930826.2021.1984142.

Wikipedia. 2022. "List of Medical Schools in the United States: Developing Medical Schools." *Wikipedia*, December 16, 2022. https://en.wikipedia.org/wiki/List_of_medical_schools_in_the_United_States#Developing_medical_schools.

5

Leadership vs Management

Gerald (Jerry) Perry

> "You never let a serious crisis go to waste. And what I mean by that is it is an opportunity to do things you think you could not do before."
>
> —Rahm Emanuel

The Need for Transformational Change

Rahm Emanuel's comment about not wasting a crisis has become a much-quoted saying, a truism about not only making the most of a dire situation but also using the crisis to enact transformational rather than incremental change. According to the 23rd White House Chief of Staff, former Chicago Mayor, and presently US Ambassador to Japan, the greater the crisis, the more substantive the opportunity to advance innovative thinking and approaches to solving the challenges of the day.

The concomitant crises of the COVID-19 pandemic and structural racism evinced by the murder of George Floyd in May 2020 and the wave of national outrage and protest that followed are twin crises the scale of which are arguably unprecedented, begging for truly transformative social, political, and cultural change, including change at work.

These crises can be seen as tipping points, rushing to the fore a level of change in our work environments that, for the strategic leader, can be leveraged not only for contemporary success but also lasting impact. They afford the reflective leader a framing and rationale to drive transformational change at the workplace, advancing both the mission of the organization and the success of staff who choose to work for the organization. Why change? Because the twin crises have shown us that the nature of how we work, and the nature of our workplaces and work cultures, are outmoded and threaten our success.

Key Points

In this chapter of a book about managing health sciences libraries during a time of change, the author argues that a reflective, strategic library director or dean can bring about substantive, transformational change in their library through strategic planning, through centering their management practice in a model that is inclusive and appreciative, and through understanding the changing dynamics around attitudes and approaches to work among library workers. The key points of this chapter are:

- Planning to manage change and learning from our collective past;
- Centering your leadership in a practice model; and
- Understanding the changing nature of work.

These key points are used to structure the text that follows.

Planning to Manage Change: Lessons from Published Literature

For directors and deans of health sciences libraries, there is a strong corpus of texts that should be read and can be consulted on best practices for managing and leading the library. These volumes outline the core functions of the library, including planning, budgeting, human resources management, outreach and advocacy, assessment, and systems and approaches for continuous quality improvement. Perhaps not surprisingly, all posit the library in a time of rapid and inexorable change, and they reflect the eras in which they were written.

In the Medical Library Association-sponsored series "Current Practice in Health Sciences Librarianship," by Alison Bunting, editor-in-chief, Volume 8 on *Administration and Management in Health Sciences Libraries* (2000) is a standout for its thoroughness, thoughtfulness, and depth of reflection. Edited by Rick Forsman, two chapters are particularly noteworthy as they frame the drivers of change during the periods in which they were published and are particularly relevant to the key points of this chapter.

In their chapter "Management Challenges in an Era of Change: An Overview," Epstein, Mickelson, and Detlefsen focus on the economic disruptions surrounding healthcare reform in the United States and the impact this was having in the healthcare delivery environment, wherein the health sciences library was faced with the existential crisis of surviving the transition from print to digital, demonstrating the value proposition of the library during a period of significant economic retraction and financial adjustments in the healthcare delivery marketplace.

Reflecting the same crisis-as-opportunity mantra espoused by Emanuel, they wrote, "Rapid advances in technological development create both unprecedented opportunities and enormous dilemmas for library managers in health care settings." They continue, "The successful manager will see these changes as opportunities for increased institution-wide integration and not as insurmountable or discouraging impediments. Strong management skills will enable library administrators to succeed in this volatile environment."

Framing the existential threat, they note, "Libraries in particular may face the real risk of being perceived as luxurious anachronisms replaceable by hardware and software run by end users, such as clinicians and researchers working with integrated information systems at their desks and in their clinical examination rooms." Their advice to the director or dean is dynamism and the ability to quickly pivot: "Library managers must critically and periodically reevaluate their administrative structures, service delivery mechanisms, collection development, computer systems, budget allocation, staffing patterns, and physical space to adapt to their new institutional environment."

The dynamism they promote speaks to the role of the director or dean as strategic leader who is nonetheless focused on operational goals. They do not explicitly address the tension between leadership versus management, wherein leadership is seen as directing the strategic through visioning, whereas management is seen as fulfilling the day-to-day operational needs of the organization. Their advice:

> Few clear-cut rules exist for attaining success as a manager during times of rapid and pervasive change. Instead, a mix of knowledge and skills is essential. An understanding of management principles and theories, coupled with knowledge of the institutional environment, a strong working

relationship with other units in the institution, effective personal communication skills, well-developed political skills, good judgement, and the ability to flourish in a dynamic environment constitute a promising formula for a fruitful and rewarding management career.

That same pragmatic approach is reflected in the book's chapter "Human Resources Management," authored by Jenkins. Also reflecting on change, Jenkins argues, "As the roles of health sciences libraries change to meet the needs of their clientele, it is vital that the library administrator maximize the value of the library staff within the parent organization. In today's rapidly changing environment, achieving the maximum contribution by the staff requires careful attention to all aspects of the human resources management process." Jenkins carefully reviews the core tasks for human resources management but is particularly prescient in her reflections on the retention of qualified staff. She notes, "Recruiting and hiring the best possible staff represents the essential role of the library administrator. Having made the substantial investment in recruitment, no one wants to think about staff turnover and the continuing cycle of recruitment that this implies. Certainly, the wise administrator will recognize that retention is as important a human resources role as recruitment." She goes on to note, "Retention of staff will depend on whether the library meets the staff member's expectations, and vice versa."

Key among the expectations Jenkins cites are opportunities for professional growth, compensation, and benefits; evaluating performance; and overall quality of work life. Jenkins goes on to make a compelling case for a planned, systematic staff development program. Jenkins additionally links planning efforts to performance management, evaluation, and assessment. Again, reflecting on the theme of change, Jenkins argues, "As rapid change in library roles and functions continues to affect the nature of work performed by staff at all levels, it is critical that staff participate in setting library-wide goals and shaping the specific roles of their work unit."

Addressing the context for healthy performance management, Jenkins advises that "Effective performance evaluation depends on having an atmosphere of trust and open communication in the library. This ensures that employees know on what basis they are being evaluated and how."

Foreshadowing human resource management issues with which we are living today after the twin crises of the COVID-19 pandemic and structural racism, Jenkin's chapter section on "Stress and the Quality of Work Life" is especially informative. Jenkins links planning for work performance and evaluation to the quality of work life as experienced by library workers. Jenkins writes, "In the highly demanding environment in which health sciences libraries face daily challenges of adapting services to meet constant changes in health care and technology, management strives to maintain a satisfied workforce. Administrators provide staff with a clear involvement in library decision-making and show a commitment to staff training and professional development. Both of these factors help employees feel anchored in a rapidly changing environment."

Jenkins goes on to note:

Another consideration gaining importance is alternative work patterns and schedules. For instance, teleworking from off-site is becoming a mainstream way of working. Staff are able to serve on teams or "knowledge communities" that stay in touch electronically and do not meet physically. This changes human resources strategies significantly because it can improve the quality of work life for employees who desire flexibility in work schedules and physical location.

Jenkins also makes note of the work on stress and burnout in libraries by Janette Caputo. Summarizing those contributions to our understanding of human resources management in libraries, Jenkins notes, "Surveys conducted in the 1980s confirmed that librarians were experiencing burnout to a considerable degree. The surveyors found that librarians experience many of the stressors common to members of other professions: anxiety over rapid technological changes, budget cuts, heavy workloads, poor management, obnoxious patrons, shifting priorities, discrimination, lack of involvement in decision making, and working nights and weekends."

The same pragmatism evinced in the leadership and management advice contained in the Forsman-edited work can be found in the almost encyclopedic scale and scope of editors Bandy and Dudden's *The Medical Library Association Guide to Managing Health Care Libraries* (2011). Cautioning the library director or dean to embrace both the strategic and operational nature of leadership, authors Donaldson and Wellik write, in the chapter "Topics in Management,"

> Where managers hold process, stability, and control as valuable, and seek quick solutions to problems, leaders embrace chaos and a lack of structure so they can take advantage of the situation and fully understand existing issues that have created the problem. Librarians need to embrace both concepts. The speed at which the library world is changing mandates that today's librarian see quick solutions and seek a greater level of understanding, simultaneously serving as both leader and manager, changing hats quite often.

Donaldson and Wellik's dynamic form of pragmatism is reflected in their grounding of the management of libraries in planning processes. They advise, "As health care organizations face change and unpredictable futures, effective planning plays an important role in the library achieving its purpose of providing information services to meet the needs of customers. Strategic planning is a tool that allows the library to evolve its products and services in a systematic fashion, taking into account the types of information needed by library users as well as the best way to deliver it." They go on to describe in detail the steps for planning, including the groundwork that must be done to prepare the organization for the planning process.

Cunningham's chapter "Library Administration in Health Sciences Libraries" in *Health Sciences Librarianship* (2000), edited by Sandra Wood, introduces the reader to a range of management theories and models from "Benevolent Neglect" and Herzberg's Theory of Motivation to Senge's work on Learning Organizations, management by objectives to participatory management and strategic management. She links this last model of management to the planning processing, noting, "The strategic management approach creates a vision of the future, sets objectives, and lays out the day-to-day activities needed to reach this vision. Communicating the vision to others is critical, involving staff in the process and inspiring them to see a vision and make it happen. Developing a strategic plan is the result of this management approach."

Cunningham addresses the role of the director or dean in managing "up," "down," and sideways, referring to the roles of managing up the chain of command or your bosses, the individuals you are leading, and the relationships you have with peer leaders. She also stresses the roles of developing the next generation of leaders and of mentoring others for success. Cunningham states, "Managers need to understand and learn about their employees as individuals, to empathize with differing points of view and show that they care about employees' progress." Citing Rachel Singer Gordon, Cunningham notes, "Most employees quit their managers, not their jobs." This is a prescient insight, knowing what we have learned from the "Great Resignation" phenomenon of the COVID-19 pandemic era.

According to the Pew Research Center, "The COVID-19 pandemic set off nearly unprecedented churn in the U.S. labor market. Widespread job losses in the early months of the pandemic gave way to tight labor markets in 2021, driven in part by what's come to be known as the Great Resignation. The nation's 'quit rate' reached a 20-year high last November." A Pew Research Center survey (2023) subsequently found that low pay, a lack of opportunities for advancement, and feeling disrespected at work were the top reasons given as to why Americans quit their jobs. In a tight labor market, employees have choices, which can mean that a toxic relationship with a supervisor or leader no longer needs to be tolerated.

The throughlines of all these works are a strong grounding in strategic visioning and planning, a recognition of the persistence of change and the need for flexibility and agility, a *dynamic pragmatism* that frames the leadership experience, and a recognition that the library will only be as successful as the team that makes up its staff. Each is an informative read for the novice and experienced director or dean, providing a grounding in the culture and environment of health sciences library leadership. In the end, however, it will be incumbent on the director or dean to recognize their own skills and capacity and to identify a model or approach that aligns with their values, their outlook on leadership, and their understanding of the role of the leader. All that is critical for reflective practice.

Centering Your Leadership in a Practice Model

A model of leadership that combines a reflective process while recognizing the diversity of assets at hand to aid the leader is appreciative inquiry. Much has been written about this approach, but as the author understands and uses this model, it is a process whereby the leader engages with stakeholders to understand their interests, strengths, and assets, along with what it is they wish to do and learn, and then applies that learning by matching individuals with opportunities to lead, to investigate their interests, grow their strengths, and learn what interests and drives them. It is the role of the leader to coordinate these interests and talents and to set a course of action for the collective based on an understanding of the strengths, but also gaps, that exist within the working team. The leader works to shore up any gaps while encouraging and promoting a vision for the organization.

A second key step for success with this management model is being fully versed in and aware of the mission of the organization and why it exists, what its functions are, and who it is intended to serve. The mission provides both a point of departure for the team's work while also serving as a familiar port to which the team can return repeatedly, as work opportunities and challenges are met and addressed. Familiarity with the mission is a critical step in the strategic planning process that almost always starts with an articulation of the mission, vision, and values of the organization.

As with knowing and returning to the mission, knowing, working within, and returning to a management practice model provides a point of departure and a port to which to return, centering and grounding the leader and the organization through change. Planning for change can be achieved through the inherent flexibility of the appreciative inquiry model, which allows the leader to stop, assess, reflect, and advance while grounded in the quantitative and qualitative evidence derived from the inquiry process, which entails engagement and conversation with stakeholders—interviewing and discussing to achieve understanding. Having a clear and pragmatically based understanding of the realities of library work grounded in evidence is necessary for managing and leading through change.

Understanding the Changing Nature of Work

It is early in the present twin crises era of the COVID-19 pandemic and the national reckoning over structural racism. The research is yet to be conducted, but we have evidence based on the lived experiences of people and reports in the media that signals a "new normal" for work emerging.

With the onset of the COVID-19 pandemic, all but essential workers were required to work from home to avoid additional morbidity and mortality from the coronavirus variants that swept the globe. In this fraught environment, the world watched while George Floyd, yet another Black man, was killed by police in Minneapolis, his death captured on video that was widely shared via social media platforms. Many across the nation rose in protest, leading to a level of recognition of the ongoing injustice of structural racism not seen since the Civil Rights era.

These twin crises have led to new insights and understandings about the changing nature of work. While this is not the case for all professions, we learned that individuals could work from home if equipped with the necessary broadband infrastructure, telecommunications resources, computing devices, and communications technologies, such as Zoom. We learned that some individuals could be particularly productive working from home, and not having to commute provided a source of relief for families and individuals balancing the needs of work with childcare, elder care, personal health needs, and other incumbencies. Their quality of life was enhanced by this approach, leading many to resist the return to the office. Ample stories in national media have documented the changing nature of work as companies, the public sector, and nonprofits have struggled with the where and when to work as the COVID-19 pandemic recedes.

Concomitantly, the significantly greater visibility during the pandemic of structural racism with which we have lived for so long has called many to question fundamentals of work life, from recruitment to retention, staff development to promotion. How and why have historically based practices prevented Black, Indigenous and People of Color (BIPOC) from advancing at work? Along with that questioning has come the phenomenon known in the media as the "Great Resignation." According to the Society for Human Resources Management (SHRM), in 2021, almost forty-eight million workers quit their jobs, leaving many businesses scrambling for sufficiently qualified workers. That massive departure of talent has left many businesses reeling to find workers, but it also has emboldened employees.

Workers have discovered a level of power that comes with an employment market where the demand is greater than the supply. Qualified employees now have a level of choice that has not been experienced in many decades, and they can set terms that challenge the work organization to be more transparent and equitable. Businesses are adopting innovative approaches to interviewing, new ways of accounting for experience, and are considering new strategies for retaining workers once they have committed to working for an organization. These approaches auger well for a more fair and equitable work experience for all employees.

Libraries are not immune to these phenomena, and we see through the diversity, equity, inclusion, and antiracism efforts of organizations like the Medical Library Association and the Association of Academic Health Sciences Libraries' commitments to address these emerging dynamics in our libraries as places of work. Leaders of libraries must attend to these new dynamics and the emerging new normal state of work life to ensure that progress towards mission and the fulfillment of strategic plans can be achieved with a qualified workforce that has the needed talents but also equitable opportunities to achieve. Here the appreciative inquiry process can be an especially helpful tool as it is through appreciative interviewing processes that the leader comes to know the barriers and challenges that individuals face in their work journey. The leader can reflect and subsequently practice the dynamic pragmatism for which leadership of health sciences libraries has been marked.

Concluding Notes of Hope and Caution

Reflecting on the Emanuel quote that launched this chapter, "You never let a serious crisis go to waste. And what I mean by that it is an opportunity to do things you think you could not do before," the new normal post-COVID-19 pandemic and the ongoing reckoning with historically based structural racism are twin crises the scale of which most of us could not have fathomed but which afford opportunities for leaders to evolve and pivot with new realities. Pardoning the pun, health sciences libraries are not immune to the changes wrought by the twin crises. Nor are their leaders exempt from the needed reckoning that is coming, exacerbated by these events but with long roots in our collective past.

Emerging scholarship by Kendrick, as published in the *Journal of Library Administration* on "The Low Morale Experience of Academic Librarians: A Phenomenological Study," and the 2019 University of San Diego dissertation by Alma Ortega, "Academic Libraries and Toxic Leadership," are illuminating problems that have existed for an exceedingly long time in many of our libraries. These scholars, as well as leaders in the critical librarianship movement, are casting light on issues not often addressed in the library leadership literature and call the leader to respond. Why is it that so many library workers experience low morale, and why is it that toxic leaders can persist in library organizations? What can we learn from understanding the new emerging power dynamics that exist when workers have greater choices about where and with whom to work and when our workplaces are subject to critical assessment and review, sometimes revealing structural components that mitigate against the success of staff?

Ortega's dissertation documents the experience of toxic leadership in libraries and starts a conversation about the presence of this phenomenon, how it is expressed, and the impacts it has leading to low morale and impacting the commitment of workers to the mission of libraries and our profession.

Kendrick's work helps us start to understand the long-term consequences of workplace abuse on the mental and physical health of workers, the systemic features of organizations that enable trauma to workers, and the potential long-term impacts of these experiences on careers in librarianship.

One particularly problematic long-term aspect of the profession, vocational awe, was described by Fobazi Ettarh in a 2018 article in the open-access journal *In the Library with the Lead Pipe*. Ettarh describes this phenomenon as "the set of ideas, values, and assumptions librarians have about themselves and the profession that result in notions that libraries as institutions are inherently good, sacred notions, and therefore beyond critique." The article is a must-read, especially for leaders and managers in all libraries, as it provides insights into how historical conceptualizations of the library and library work have facilitated the ongoing structural oppression of library workers, primarily women. Critical appraisal and awareness of these concepts are discussed now at professional meetings and conferences. Leaders cannot assume that the ongoing chronic underfunding of libraries and the precarity of library work are not recognized by employees. Reflective leaders must understand these dynamics and the implication for the profession and for their libraries.

These are important research trajectories that must be supported and advanced. Such scholarship will be necessary to ensure that the pragmatic dynamism evinced by our profession and the practice models that support leadership through change continue into the new normal and hopefully post-twin-crises era and remain salient and valuable hallmarks of the profession and of the reflective leader.

Discussion Questions

1. Reflecting on the emerging post-pandemic new normal for work, how might flexible approaches to where, when, and how library workers perform their work impact the mission of the library?
2. How might the health sciences library leader plan for the quality of dynamic pragmatism in their leadership style and approach?
3. What can health sciences library leaders do within a model of management and leadership to help avoid the challenge and negative long-term impacts of low morale in the workplace?

Recommended Readings

Health Education England, National Health Service, United Kingdom. 2019–2021. "The Topol Review: Preparing the Healthcare Workforce to Deliver the Digital Future." https://topol.hee.nhs.uk/.

Rieger, Oya Y. October 2020. "Academic Health Sciences Libraries: Structural Models and Perspectives." Ithaka S&R. https://sr.ithaka.org/publications/academic-health-science-libraries/.

Works Cited

"About MLA." Medical Library Association. Accessed May 20, 2022. https://www.mlanet.org/p/cm/ld/fid=21.

"Ambassador Rahm Emanuel." U.S. Embassy and Consulates in Japan. Accessed January 17, 2023. https://jp.usembassy.gov/ambassador-rahm-emanuel/.

Bandy, Margaret Moylan, and Rosalind Farnam Dudden, eds. 2011. *The Medical Library Association Guide to Managing HealthCare Libraries,* 2nd ed. New York: Neal-Schuman Publishers.

Caputo, Janette S. 1991. *Stress and Burnout in Library Service*. Phoenix, AZ: Oryx Press, 60.

Cook, Ian. 2021. "Who Is Driving the Great Resignation?" *Harvard Business Review: Human Resource Management*, September 15, 2021. Accessed January 17, 2023. https://hbr.org/2021/09/who-is-driving-the-great-resignation.

Cunningham, Diana J. 2014. "Library Administration in Health Sciences libraries." In M. Sandra Wood, ed. *Health Sciences Librarianship*, 353–63. Lanham, MD: Rowman & Littlefield.

Doyle, Jacqueline Donaldson, and Kay E. Wellik. "Topics in Management." In Margaret Moylan Bandy and Rosalind Farnam Dudden, eds. *The Medical Library Association Guide to Managing Health Care Libraries, 2nd ed.*, 38–42. New York: Neal-Schuman, 2011.

Epstein, Barbara A., Patricia C. Mickelson, and Ellen G. Detlefsen. 2000. "Management Challenges in an Era of Change: An Overview." In Rick B. Forsman, ed. *Volume 8, Administration and Management in Health Sciences Libraries. Current Practice in Health Sciences Librarianship*, 1–17. Lanham, MD: Medical Library Association and the Scarecrow Press.

Forsman, Rick B, ed. 2000. *Volume 8, Administration and Management in Health Sciences Libraries. Current Practice in Health Sciences Librarianship*. Lanham, MD: Medical Library Association and the Scarecrow Press.

Gordon, Rachel Singer. 2006. "Seven Deadly Sins (and Desirable Strategies) for Library Mangers," *FreePint* 196. January 5, 2006. Accessed May 20, 2022. https://www.jinfo.com/library/issues/050106.pdf.

"Healthcare Crisis: Healthcare Timeline." Public Broadcasting System (PBS). Accessed January 17, 2023. https://www.pbs.org/healthcarecrisis/history.htm.

"How George Floyd Died, and What Happened Next." *The New York Times*, July 29, 2022. Accessed January 17, 2023. https://www.nytimes.com/article/george-floyd.html.

"Interactive Chart: How Historic has the Great Resignation Been?" Society for Human Resources Management (SHRM). Accessed May 20, 2022. https://www.shrm.org/resourcesandtools/hr-topics/talent-acquisition/pages/interactive-quits-level-by-year.aspx.

Jenkins, Carol. 2000. "Human Resources Management." In Rick B. Forsman, ed. *Volume 8, Administration and Management in Health Sciences Libraries. Current Practice in Health Sciences Librarianship*, 35–73. Lanham, MD: Medical Library Association and the Scarecrow Press.

"Leadership Vs. Management: What's the Difference." Business Insights, Harvard Business School Online. Accessed May 20, 2022, https://online.hbs.edu/blog/post/leadership-vs-management.

Parker, Kim, and Juliana Menasce Horowitz. 2022. "Majority of Workers who Quit a Job in 2021 Cite Low Pay, No Opportunities for Advancement, Feeling Disrespected." Pew Research Center: Numbers, Facts and Trends Shaping Your World, March 9, 2022. Accessed January 17, 2023. https://www.pewresearch.org/fact-tank/2022/03/09/majority-of-workers-who-quit-a-job-in-2021-cite-low-pay-no-opportunities-for-advancement-feeling-disrespected/.

"Rahm Emanuel Quotes (6)." IMDb. Accessed February 6, 2023. https://m.imdb.com/name/nm0256043/quotes.

"The Big Question: Is the World of Work Forever Changed." *The New York Times*, December 8, 2021. Accessed January 17, 2023. https://www.nytimes.com/2021/12/08/special-series/pandemic-future-work-lifestyle.html.

"What Is Appreciative Inquiry? A Short Guide to the Appreciative Inquiry Model and Process," Center for Values-Driven Leadership, Benedictine University. Accessed January 17, 2023. https://cvdl.ben.edu/blog/what-is-appreciative-inquiry/.

"What Is Coronavirus?" Johns Hopkins Medicine, updated July 29, 2022. Accessed January 17, 2023. https://www.hopkinsmedicine.org/health/conditions-and-diseases/coronavirus.

6

Management Skills for the Successful Library Leader

Claire B. Joseph

> . . . be not afraid of greatness. Some are become / great, some achieve greatness, and some have greatness thrust / upon 'em
>
> —Shakespeare. *Twelfth Night*, Act 2, Scene 5, lines 125–28

Key Points

Leadership. What is the definition of a leader? There is a plethora (or is it a myriad?) of responses to that question. What attributes and skill sets does a leader need to possess? And are such abilities obtainable through education and experience, or does one have to be a "natural born" leader? And specifically, what makes a library leader, or more precisely, a health sciences library leader?

A Brief Note on Leadership versus Management

(The previous chapter in this book discussed this at length.)

There are definite distinctions between the jobs of a library director and a library manager. A director, whose position can be likened to a movie director or the conductor of an orchestra, must certainly be skilled at their position and knowledgeable of everyone else's, but their focus is on the "big picture." Directors are attuned to the culture of their organizations, and they align their library with those goals. A library manager, on the other hand, usually manages, or is in charge of, the administration of a specific group of library personnel, a specific library department or function, or a specific library project, or some combination of the above. It's interesting to note that some of the responsibilities required of a library manager are similar to those of a library leader. They can include library administration, strategic planning, program planning, planning implementation and evaluation, project coordination, and grant oversight. These are broad areas that require cooperation of staff and stakeholders.

Sometimes the terms leader and manager are used interchangeably, and it can be confusing and perhaps a matter of semantics when it comes to how a job title is indicated. Some larger libraries will speak of "middle management," or managers, but will refer to the library director position as "upper management." Freedman and Freedman (2017) offer an excellent summation of the differences: "A simple differentiating factor is that leaders are usually in the position of deciding what is to be done in any situation. A manager is principally concerned with how things will be done once such decision are made. While managers may from time to time exercise leadership in various aspects of their role, strategic decision-making is the primary role and responsibility of leaders."

For the purposes of this chapter, it is posited that all librarians who are in a position to oversee, direct, or lead employees may be referred to as "leaders," and certainly good leadership principles apply to them all.

How does one get to be a library leader? There are those who have a clear-cut goal to follow a career pathway to leadership. Then there are those librarians who, through time and circumstance—or luck—find themselves at a library that offers training opportunities, formal or informal, that set them on the leadership pathway. And then there are those who have leadership "thrust upon 'em" due to some unforeseen job vacancy.

Any librarian interested in becoming a library leader can do so! This chapter will explore the various skills, attributes, and personal characteristics necessary to be or become an effective leader and how they may be learned and acquired, whether it be by recognizing and teasing out one's existing capabilities or potential by recognizing and pursuing positions that offer opportunities to develop skills most needed for leadership, or by pursuing academic training opportunities, or by mentorship experiences, or by some combinations thereof.

What is the definition of a leader? Martin (2020) observes that, in fact, "No agreed upon definition of leadership exists," and furthermore, "to some extent, leadership is in the eye of the beholder," and in addition "every library leader has their own leadership style, approach, and practice." However, Freedman and Freedman (2017) "propose a simple definition that leadership is the ability to influence the behavior of others to achieve team, group, or organizational goals."

A particularly perceptive definition of leadership comes from the National Library of Medicine's Medical Subject Headings (MeSH), which defines leadership as: "The function of directing or controlling the actions or attitudes of an individual or group with more or less willing acquiescence of the followers" (ncbi.nlm.nih.gov/mesh/?term=leadership).

"More or less willing acquiescence of the followers" underscores not only that leading staff can be, at times, like herding cats, but it would also seem to subtly suggest that there is no such thing as a "perfect" leader. This also brings into play the concept of "followership," or, very simply put, the willingness to follow a leader. As Martin (2018) observes, "Followers play an important role in the leadership process. They choose whom to follow and whom not to follow."

Any librarian interested in pursuing a leadership position needs to begin by asking themselves, "What type of leader do I want to be? What type of leader do I need to be?" Self-understanding and self-awareness of skills, attributes, and personality traits are basic starting points. In addition, a leader or future leader needs to possess excellence in the field of librarianship and must thoroughly understand the culture (e.g., the shared identity, goals, norms, and expected behaviors) and needs of the library they hope to lead; they also need to understand the culture of the larger organizations of which they most likely are a part, as most health sciences libraries are rarely entities unto themselves. Health sciences library leaders, be they solo librarians in hospitals, directors of health sciences libraries of multisite healthcare organizations, or directors of health sciences libraries in medical/nursing/allied health schools or other academic settings, all share the need to not only have the capacity to effectively lead their staff but also to effectively interact with campus or healthcare departments, including the institution's administrative offices.

Some Leadership Theories

An effective leader needs to not only possess knowledge-based skills but also "people skills," or emotional intelligence. As Martin (2020) emphasizes, "Library leaders should have a mission first, people always mindset."

Capdarest-Arest (2020) notes, "Leadership and the theory behind what makes leaders 'leaders' is a complex and intermingled topic." While there are innumerable theories and philosophies of leadership, or frameworks, in general and in library leadership specifically, the following is a sampling of some of the more popular ones.

Transformational Leadership

- Characterized by charismatic influence, effective communication, valorization of relationships, and individualized considerations (Specchia, 1-2).
- The 4 "I's" of "Transformational Leadership"(Michigan State University):

  1. Intellectual Stimulation
  2. Individual Consideration
  3. Inspirational Motivation
  4. Idealized Influence

Contingency Leadership

- Not all leaders are right for all situations.
- A leader must be the right fit for an organization and its current situation.
- Leaders are more effective at either being Task Leaders or Relations Leaders; very few leaders are effective at both.
- An organization needs different leaders at different times.
- Culture plays a large role in determining leader fit.

Situational Leadership

- Leaders adapt leadership style to follower's ability.
- Leaders assign tasks based on ability and experience.
- Job complexity is a critical part of job satisfaction.
- Job should be challenging but still within reach.
- Requires leaders to understand others' technical competence and career goals (Martin, 2020).

Servant Leadership

- Put needs of others first, "other-oriented."
- Focus on the strength of the team, helping all achieve goals.
- Develop trust by listening and empathy ("soft skills").
- Build community.

How do you determine the best leadership framework to follow? This requires leaders to not only take a thorough "inventory" of their traits, skills, and abilities—or lack thereof—but to also, perhaps intuitively, understand the culture of their institution and acquire a full knowledge of staff and their specific duties. This can take time, of course, but prior experience and training, not to mention an open mind and a willingness to listen to staff, will be invaluable. As Freedman and Freedman (2017) advise, "To be especially effective, leaders must listen broadly and well, ask questions, develop the skills of the people they lead and develop other leaders."

Attaining Library Leadership Skills

Knowledge-Based Skills

The librarian who aspires to library leadership needs, in effect, to recognize and work to achieve or enhance and nurture both knowledge-based skills and "people skills." The Medical Library Association (MLA) emphasizes "Professional Competencies" and created a Task Force to review "MLA Competencies for Lifelong Learning and Professional Success" to "identify essential professional skills and abilities that can be observed, measured, and taught" (https://www.mlanet.org/page/test-competencies). Their "Competency 4: Leadership & Management" is shown in Table 6.1.

In addition to these prescribed leadership skills and abilities, it is also interesting to contemplate more broadly defined "ideal" qualities of library leaders. Chow and Rich (2013) conducted a study where they interviewed 114 academic, public, school media, and special library administrators over a one-year period (p. 21). They found "that there are four major factors identified by library administrators as ideal qualities across different types of libraries: empathy, vision, communication, and flexibility. . . . Four additional factors . . . included delegation, creativity, integrity, and passion." These factors are a mix of tangible skills and intangible emotional intelligence and "soft skills."

Along with MLA continuing education courses and programs, "leadership skills can be achieved through coursework in an MLIS program, life experiences, work experiences, or a combination of these." Interestingly, Wong (2017) maintains that "leadership capabilities are nurtured through experience and practice" and points out the merits of "on-the-job" development (p. 9). Camille and Westbrook (2013) describe a program created at the University of Houston Libraries, the "Excellence in Library Leadership Program" (p. 447). The impetus was the realization that "few libraries can afford to hire new leaders to head teams, manage people and projects effectively, and contribute to the vision and direction of the organization" and instead opted to "increase the leadership skills of the talented librarians and staff members already working in their libraries."

Communication and Emotional Intelligence

Along with knowledge-based skills developed in formal courses or "on the job," library leaders must also possess and develop relational skills, "soft skills," along with emotional intelligence, or interpersonal or "people skills."

While it might seem self-evident to treat people according to the "Golden Rule" maxim—to treat others as one would like oneself to be treated—when it comes to creating a workplace culture of mutual respect, honesty, integrity, and job effectiveness, along with ensuring and promoting a culture of diversity, equity, and inclusion, one must take the time to reflect on one's soft skills and emotional intelligence.

Emotional intelligence (EI) can be defined as "the capacity to be aware of, control, and express one's emotions, and to handle interpersonal relationships effectively within your library" (Lucas, p. 1). An important component of EI is empathy, the ability to understand the feelings of others, to "feel their pain." As Lucas (2020) emphasizes, "Understanding yourself and looking objectively at your strengths and areas for improvement is the first step to take in developing and improving EI." (p. 5).

Soft skills fall under the umbrella of relational and communication skills (Matteson, et al., 428). Library leaders "need . . . to be highly effective at leadership, outreach, collaboration . . . advocate for resources, negotiate with vendors and administrators, and build relationships and provide social support . . . all these roles require relational or 'soft skills'—the non-technical, interpersonal abilities used to facilitate work and achieve goals." Library leaders need not be great orators, but they do need to speak effectively and be clearly understood by the many people and groups they must interact with, including staff and administration. Farrell (2017) suggests that "Leaders also learn public presentation skills to tell a story quickly in order to maximize time constraints with busy officials or boards. Such

Table 6.1. MLA Competency 4: Leadership & Management

Indicator	Basic	Expert
Strategically organizes people and resources to serve institutional needs.	Identifies goals; initiates, plans, and delegates tasks to meet goals; analyzes and communicates outcomes to relevant stakeholders; fosters a positive team environment; serves as team member role model.	Establishes, justifies, and leads large-scale collaborative projects that demonstrate return on investment to stakeholders; provides and models value-based leadership through staff and resource administration.
Creates and implements strategic plans.	Describes the strategic planning process.	Creates and implements strategic plans.
Inspires and leads others to perform at their highest level.	Uses communication and collaboration skills.	Articulates a vision, motivates and leads others to contribute to realization of the vision, and guides institutional change.
Integrates multicultural awareness and appreciation of diversity and equality into professional practice.	Describes own cultural background and recognizes biases; values cultural norms, experiences of others, and expressions of diverse viewpoints; recognizes power dynamics in relationships.	Develops and implements practices that foster diversity and equality; contributes to correcting inequities; participates in external collaborations.
Practices fiscal accountability and stewardship and follows institutional resource policies.	Describes established policies that safeguard assets consistent with institutional objectives and sound business principles.	Controls and supervises library resources consistent with institutional objectives and sound business principles; advocates for and secures institutional support to ensure maintenance and growth of the library.
Secures and manages external funding.	Describes grant and other external funding processes; identifies funding opportunities.	Applies grant-writing principles and strategies; identifies partners and collaborates to develop proposals; executes fundraising strategies; disseminates information about successful strategies and outcomes.

(continued)

Table 6.1: *Continued*

Indicator	Basic	Expert
Develops and implements enhancements to the library user experience.	Describes the literature on library user experience and user experience assessment.	Uses results of formal and informal user experience assessments to propose and implement library user experience enhancements.
Identifies emerging technologies and advocates for their use.	Explores and evaluates emerging technologies.	Leads initiatives to incorporate new technologies.
Allocates space and facilities.	Describes common library functions and associated space; identifies standards for space and facilities allocation.	Proposes or leads design of library facilities.
Develops and implements effective advocacy, marketing, and communication strategies.	Promotes institutional mission and goals; forms internal partnerships.	Designs marketing and public relations strategies and programs; forms external partnerships.

techniques can be adopted by an organization for productive meetings and communication that will manage the time well for all employees" (Farrell, 220).

It's also a good idea for library leaders—or anyone for that matter—to remember the power of humility. Humility is a trait that effective leaders will cultivate, as it's "an imperative leadership attribute" that can, among other things, make leaders approachable and empathetic.

Time Management

Whether a library promotes a homegrown leader or hires from outside, the vast majority of library leaders will be those librarians with professional experience. The seeds of many of the skills needed to be an effective library leader are planted during those experiences, albeit on a smaller scale, including time management.

Time management is, arguably, a skill that all aspire to, and it's something that librarians strive to master, to a greater or lesser extent, throughout both their professional and personal lives. Many speak of having the ability to "multi-task," which is one way to manage one's time more efficiently. Librarians face and must learn to adequately respond to any number of demands on their time; this can be done by assessing one's duties and prioritizing them. Of course, the higher one goes in the library, the more their responsibilities mount. Along with a multitude of books and articles on library leadership in general, there are innumerable books and articles on time management, both for libraries and in general—not surprisingly in today's fast-paced world. But, paradoxically, "leaders . . . lack the time to figure out all the time saving strategies!" (Farrell, p. 216).

As Farrell observes, "There are no perfect solutions and how one individual is able to manage their time is quite different from a successful model of another individual" (p. 217). As with any aspect of library leadership, arriving at a time-management system that works best for an individual leader begins with an assessment and full understanding of the leader's responsibilities and the library's culture. "In juggling multiple tasks and responsibilities, individuals will have a better sense of what is important if they know the vision and goals of the organization to help them focus on priority projects." Farrell recommends a "time audit."

Any "time audit" would include prioritizing one's duties; this should include a delegation of tasks. For example, does a library director need to read and personally answer each and every email they receive? Or are there categories of emails that can be directed to the director's administrative assistant and/or staff librarians? And, of course, every time audit or time-management plan should include the ability to be flexible, as time demands will ebb and flow.

The ability to effectively communicate with staff is a skill that leaders need—throughout their professional life—and this also impacts time management. Is the library involved in a major project? The director needs to let everyone know this as it will definitely impinge on the leader's time. And leaders should include professional development time (Farrell 2017, 220) and personal time in their time-management strategy.

Mentoring

Those familiar with Homer's *Odyssey* will recall Mentor, the old and trusted friend of the epic's hero, Odysseus, who, when he went off to fight in the Trojan War, placed the care and education of his son, Telemachus, along with the care of his home, with Mentor, hence the meaning of a mentor as an older (and/or more-experienced) and wiser person sharing wisdom and knowledge with a less-experienced colleague. While it is certainly possible to learn from all of one's professional colleagues, mentorship is a special experience that offers an excellent pathway to leadership.

The Association of Academic Health Sciences Libraries (AAHSL), in conjunction with the National Library of Medicine (NLM), offers the NLM/AAHSL Leadership Fellows Program that "prepares emerging leaders for the position of library director in academic health sciences libraries. . . . They are paired with mentors who are academic health sciences library Directors" (https://www.aahsl.org/leadershipfellowsprogram).

The MLA, as part of its desire to advance professional development, sponsors a mentorship program. MLA members can volunteer as mentors or find a suitable mentor. Mentoring options are grouped by areas of expertise and include Administration, Association, Education, Professional Issues, Public Services, Research, Special Librarianship, Technical Services, and Technology (https://www.mlanet.org/page/mentoring).

Of course, there are also less structured pathways to attaining leadership skills and positions. The wise and perceptive librarian can proactively seek, by observation and by approaching senior staff members, to learn all that they can about leadership positions and what skills are needed. And often, libraries will offer opportunities to develop their staff's leadership skills for success planning for the library's future.

Library Leadership and the "New Normal"

Recent societal events have shaken the country to its core and torn at the very moral and ethical fabric of its collective culture. The killing in 2020 of George Floyd by a police officer, and other similar egregious events, served to shine a harsh light on systemic racism in the United States, inspiring the MLA and its communities—and many other organizations—to officially condemn systemic racism, violence, and hatred and to support, foster, and nurture diversity, equity, and inclusion. Of course, the ideals and goals behind these statements need to be placed into action. And this includes library leadership actively offering staff education on implicit bias, or unconscious or involuntary biases. While implicit bias may be unconscious or involuntary, its effects are very real.

Along with staff education in implicit bias, library leaders will actively offer education in cultural humility, or cultural sensitivity. This goes beyond cultural competence, which focuses on education and understanding of elements of various cultures of the communities libraries serve. Cultural humility training, like implicit bias training, focuses on self-reflection and the awareness of how librarians react to and treat those they interact with. With heightened acknowledgment and understanding, librarians will interact with colleagues and patrons alike in a manner that fosters diversity, equity, and inclusion *for all,* and leaders will strive to nurture this heightened awareness, as it is not just a "one-off" concept.

The inconceivable and never-ending spate of shootings throughout society, especially the absolutely abhorrent mass killings of children, add "active shooter" policies and procedures to the long list of responsibilities of library leaders.

Libraries should be, literally and figuratively, "safe spaces" for all who use them.

The societal upheaval of the COVID-19 pandemic certainly did not spare libraries, which were turned "upside down," forcing library leaders to learn to lead in new and often unfamiliar ways (e.g., remotely), and often had to do so given twenty-four to forty-eight-hour notice.

With the COVID-19 pandemic, much has been written on the concept of resilience; NLM's MeSH defines this as "The human ability to adapt in the face of tragedy, trauma, adversity, hardship, and ongoing significant life stressors" (https://www.ncbi.nih.gov/mesh/680555000). Librarians, in particular health sciences librarians, have learned to be flexible, resilient, and open to and ready for change and whatever challenges come their way.

In 1995, MLA created a bookmark that posed the question: "What do you have to know TODAY?" This emphasizes that health sciences themselves are dynamic fields that often change seemingly at will. Health sciences librarians find a way to get things done! And good leadership skills make it all seem easy.

The position of library leader is of the greatest importance to a library, and the job rewards outweigh the great amount of skills, abilities, and hard work needed to be effective. All librarians who aspire to leadership roles can find their pathway through an open and honest self-inventory of strengths and weaknesses and a passion to take all the steps necessary, be they personal or educational, to become an effective leader.

Discussion Questions

1. If a librarian hopes to move to a leadership position, what are some of the things that can be done proactively?
2. What are some leadership theories or frameworks, and how best can librarians determine what is the best fit for their library?
3. What is emotional intelligence, and how can it be achieved?
4. In light of horrendous societal events, what training should library directors offer all their employees?

Recommended Reading

Birrell, Lori. 2020. *Developing the Next Generation of Library Leaders*. Chicago: ALA.
Martin, Jason. 2019. *Library Leadership Your Way*. Chicago: ALA.
McCafferty, Bridgit. 2021. *Library Management: A Practical Guide for Librarians*. Lanham, MD: Rowman & Littlefield.

Works Cited

Camille, Damon, and R. Nicole Westbrook. 2013. "Building a Program that Cultivates Library Leaders from Within the Organization." *The Journal of Academic Librarianship* 39: 447–50.
Capdarest-Arest, Nicole, and Jamie M. Gray. 2020. "Health Sciences Library Leadership Skills in an Interprofessional Landscape: A Review and Textual Analysis." *Journal of the Medical Library Association* 108, no. 4: 547–55.
Chow, Anthony S., Melissa Rich. 2013. "The Ideal Qualities and Tasks of Library Leaders: Perspectives of Academic, Public, School, and Special Library Administrators." *Library Leadership & Management* 27, no. 1/2: 1–24.

Farrell, Maggie. 2017. "Leadership Reflections: Time Management." *Journal of Library Administration* 57: 215-22.

Freedman, Shin, and Jim Freedman. 2017. "The Road to Effective Leadership." *Proceedings of the Charleston Library Conference.* https://dx.doi.org/10.5703/1288284316668.

Harris-Keith, Colleen S. 2016. "What Academic Library Leadership Lacks: Leadership Skills Directors Are Least Likely to Develop, and Which Positions Offer Development Opportunity." *The Journal of Academic Librarianship* 42: 313-18.

Lucas, Debra. 2020. "Emotional Intelligence for Librarians." *Library Leadership & Management* 34, no. 3: 1-14.

Matteson, Miriam L., Matthew McShane, and Emily Hankinson. 2019. "Soft Skills Revealed: An Examination of Relational Skills in Librarianship." *Proceedings of ACRL 2019 Conference*: 428-38.

Martin, Jason. 2018. "What Do Academic Librarians Value in a Leader? Reflections on Past Positive Library Leaders and a Consideration of Future Library Leaders." *College & Research Libraries* 79, no. 6: 799-821.

———. 2020. "Library Leadership Your Way." *The Serials Librarian* 78, no. 1-4: 9-16.

Michigan State University. 2022. "The 4 'I's' of Transformational Leadership." https://www.michiganstateuniversityonline.com/resources/leadership/4-is-of-transformational-leadership/.

Phillips, Abigail. 2014. "What Do We Mean by Library Leadership? Leadership in LIS Education." *Journal of Education for Library and Information Science* 55, no. 4: 336-44.

Specchia, Maria Lucia, Maria Rosario Cozzolino, Elletra Carini, Andrea DiPilla, Caterina Galletti, Walter Ricciardi, and Gianfranco Damiana. 2021. "Leadership Styles and Nurses' Job Satisfaction. Results of a Systematic Review." *International Journal of Environmental Research and Public Health* 18: 1552-66.

Stith-Flood, Charlotte. 2018. "It's Not Hard to be Humble: The Role of Humility in Leadership." *FPM* 25, no. 3: 25-27.

Wong, Gabriella Ka Wait. 2017. "Leadership and Leadership Development in Academic Libraries: A Review." *Library Management* 38, no. 2/3: 153-66.

7

Mentoring Roles for the Library Manager

Tara Douglas-Williams and Sandra G. Franklin

Mentoring is a valuable resource that provides staff with a means to develop the skills and confidence needed for advancement to new levels of professionalism. Tara Douglas-Williams and Sandra G. Franklin present a discussion of mentoring in this chapter, examining the process of mentoring, from the viewpoint of both the mentor and the mentee. Both participants in a mentorship must be fully committed to the process—listening, training, and sharing. A successful mentorship will hopefully continue long past the actual end date of a formal program, establishing a life-long collegial relationship.

Key Points

Mentoring is:

- A life-long process that will change as you progress in your career.
- A strategic tool to help grow and develop leaders.
- A mutually beneficial, reciprocal relationship with the potential to enrich the lives of all participants.
- A highly productive approach to generating employee engagement, maintaining efficient onboarding, and intensifying career success.
- An invaluable tool to help facilitate employee and organizational accomplishments of essential goals and create a highly engaging and productive environment.

In recent years, there have been a number of unexpected and rapid changes in the landscape and normal operations of our libraries, institutions/organizations, and healthcare centers. This environment has provided opportunities for individuals in leadership to reassess their roles as leaders and explore ways to more effectively prepare current and future health sciences professionals to assume leadership roles in their careers. Mentoring is an essential tool and strategy for future health sciences leaders' recruitment, retention, and promotion. Library managers and leaders are positioned to move their organizations forward by investing time and sharing knowledge with others.

Definitions

The *Cambridge Dictionary* (2022) defines a mentor as "an experienced and trusted person who gives another person advice and help, especially related to work or school, over time." Gordon Shea delved a little deeper, defining mentoring as the following:

> A developmental, caring, sharing, and helping relationship where one person invests time, know-how, and effort in enhancing another person's growth, knowledge, and skills, and responds to critical needs in the life of that person in ways that prepare the individual for greater productivity and achievements in the future. (Shea 1994, 13)

This chapter will provide a broad overview of mentoring, tips for building a successful and long-lasting relationship, and explore the benefits mentoring provides in recruiting, retaining, and promoting librarians. The goal is to have a transformational impact on the mentee and mentor. Mentoring is one of the easiest ways to develop young leaders (Maggart and James 1999). Mentoring provides opportunities for personal, professional, and leadership development. Every library should have strategic mentoring goals that encourage connecting with others.

Mentoring

The mentor-mentee relationship is one that should be beneficial to both individuals. Both individuals should commit to being accountable, intentional, available, and honest. Expectations should be articulated clearly, and each person should be respectful of the other. The goal is to learn from each other throughout the process.

Keys to a successful mentor-mentee relationship include the following:

- Be patient.
- Be a good listener and ask questions.
- Be open to feedback and being challenged.
- Be willing to walk away if the relationship is not working favorably for you.

A key role for library leaders is to take the lead in mentoring their library employees, both professional librarians and support staff. Mentoring will encourage, motivate, and provide support to the staff members' professional development efforts, as well as provide the necessary financial support and time to engage in these activities. Eden (2017) noted that by helping staff learn, grow, and thrive, library managers will help their organizations move forward. It is essential that mentoring begin as early in one's professional life as possible. Results from a research study published in the *Journal of Applied Psychology* revealed that "people with mentors are more likely to receive promotions" (Schumer 2018). A 2015 study from the University of California-Berkeley Haas School of Business found that "women gained more social capital from affiliation with a high-status mentor than men" (Srivastava 2015).

Four Stages of the Mentoring Process

Mentoring relationships that go through the four phases of mentoring are more successful. These stages are preparation, negotiating, enabling growth, and closure. These sequential phases of mentoring build upon each other, yet they may vary in duration.

The preparation consists of getting to know each other, defining deliverables and outcomes, and exploring learning styles so that each of you feels comfortable in your new relationship.

Negotiation is composed of scheduling, creating SMART goals, and defining expectations. Negotiation facilitates clarity of what the expected outcomes will be for the mentor and mentee.

Enabling growth involves active listening, evaluating the process, and soliciting feedback. The continuous monitoring, asking questions, and the open exchange of ideas and feedback enable both the mentee and mentor to grow professionally and personally.

Mentoring can be formal or informal, depending on your options. Mentoring should be a mutually positive and reciprocal relationship that acknowledges both parties have something to offer. The mentor can learn from the mentee. It is critical that seasoned librarians, before they retire, transfer knowledge to new and mid-career librarians. This wealth of knowledge is valuable to their future success in leadership roles and vital to their understanding that new possibilities exist.

Mentoring can be delivered in various formats, such as One-On-One, Collaborative/Group, Formal, Informal, Reverse, Distance/Virtual, Peer, Team, and Flash.

Types of Mentoring

- **One-on-One:** One-on-One is the most frequently used form of mentoring, where one mentor is matched with one mentee. This is the preferred model because it allows a personal relationship to be developed and provides individual support for the mentee.
- **Collaborative/Group:** Collaborative/Group mentoring provides an opportunity for several professionals with various skills and knowledge to be directly involved in the mentoring relationship (Bynum 2015). Group mentoring requires one mentor to work with a small group (usually four to six) of mentees. The group usually meets once or twice a month to discuss diverse topics for the development of skills and knowledge.
- **Formal:** Formal mentoring is more familiar to most people. These are programs where a mentor and mentee are matched together. There is typically a specified format to adhere to, such as regular meetings, and concrete ways to track progress and monitor career development. Formal mentoring has specific objectives, measurable outcomes, time constraints, and targets that align with organizational core values. Closure marks the end of the formal stage of mentoring. At this point, the mentee and mentor should be ready to review the positive benefits of mentoring and to celebrate the growth and successes of the program (Metros 2006).
- **Informal:** Informal mentoring is more casual. Informal mentoring relationships are more organic and normally occur when a friendship already exists between the mentor and mentee. Informal mentors are great listeners, more flexible with their time, can be whomever you select, and might or might not provide expert training or be focused on specific goals.
- **Reverse:** Reverse mentoring is a form of mentoring where a junior employee is assigned to a senior employee for the purpose of providing digital and networking skills to the senior employee and business and technical guidance for the junior employee.
- **Distance/Virtual:** Distance/Virtual mentoring is becoming more popular as more people shift to working from home or other remote locations. It can take the form of one-on-one or team mentoring because it allows connecting with people without the need to meet face-to-face. The major difference is that the interactions are conducted online, yet the premise is still to form relationships through trust, empathy, and strong communication.
- **Peer:** Peer mentoring occurs when colleagues of similar ages or job levels mentor each other. This method creates a formal support system and holds colleagues accountable for their professional goals and objectives. This relationship allows colleagues to learn from one another and share advice based on past experiences. Emotional and moral support can be acquired from interactions and connections between colleagues. Peers can also provide valuable advice on balancing personal and professional responsibilities. "Mentoring Circles" can be formed to engage peers, obtain support, and build network connections.
- **Team:** Team mentoring involves a group of mentees and often multiple mentors working with the group. Team mentoring is helpful when a group is working on a shared goal or project. Team mentoring can help promote diversity, inclusion, equity, and a sense of belonging. The inclusion of people with differing opinions and perspectives creates an opportunity for team members to learn from each other.
- **Flash:** Flash mentoring refers to a type of modern mentoring that is usually a quick one-time mentoring session, meeting, or discussion aimed at learning a key piece of information or a specific skill to complete a project. This type of mentoring is valuable for creating impactful knowledge sharing, without the limitations of a long-term commitment. It can be used with group mentoring to reach more employees and to really get the most return on investment from the mentor's time.

Benefits of Mentoring

Effective mentoring requires a commitment to build a relationship and to make sure meeting times are fixed in their schedules. It is vital that the mentor and mentee remain committed and be reliable about the process throughout the relationship for it to be successful. Effective mentoring requires a commitment to create a bond and set aside scheduled time. The mentor should be a catalyst for growth and change in the mentee's life. Sustainability and flexibility are critical to the success of the mentoring relationship. Participants need to remember that sometimes life gets in the way, and alternate plans may be needed for both mentors and mentees to continue successful interactions.

Mentors and mentees must be clear on their expectations. The mentor should know whether the mentee is committed to fully developing themselves in all aspects of their professional life or in some specific facet of their professional development. Most mentees expect their mentor to share their professional and life experiences, pass on their knowledge and wisdom, and provide feedback and constructive criticism. Even if the mentor/mentee relationship is informal, it may be advisable to create an "Individual Development Plan" to identify areas of opportunity for the mentee to learn and grow. Be sure to add some stretch goals that take the mentee out of their comfort zone so they can truly experience leadership growth. Complex and diverse knowledge can be shared to inspire professional curiosity and enhance the capacity for out-of-the-box thinking. Most mentors have considerable knowledge. This is a key point that needs to be considered throughout the mentoring relationship/partnership.

Mentoring Activities

When mentoring is broken down to its core, people learn that it is all about relationships. "Mentoring activities are the intentional actions initiated by the mentor and the workplace. Mentoring practices are ingrained in the workplace through mentoring activities" (Jakubik 2016a). Welcoming, a natural and simple activity, is vital and has an impact on an employee's motivation and satisfaction (Vital and Alves 2010). A sense of belonging helps new employees become knowledgeable about the workplace and more easily assimilate into the workplace culture. Career mapping the future can serve as a critical component and conduit to opportunities and resources that prepare individuals for future positions in leadership. Career mapping can help the organization fill in succession planning gaps, as mentees self-assess and align themselves with career development opportunities (Jakubik 2016a).

Mentors reinvigorate knowledge, fill knowledge gaps, and shift the paradigm by serving as role models for leadership skills. They also encourage curiosity that leads to the creation of new knowledge. Mentors can support the transition by challenging mentees to get out of their comfort zone, listening actively, showing empathy, sharing opportunities for growth, and setting high standards for professionalism. There are many topics that can be explored during mentoring sessions, but some of the most prevalent include:

- strategic thinking
- building and nurturing teams
- problem-solving and conflict resolution
- driving impact
- effective communication
- encouraging inclusion and diversity
- emotional intelligence

Professional survival lies in having the capacity to work through organizational and situational politics. Mentors may champion the success of mentees by celebrating "mentoring moments" and creating opportunities to gain experience through role-play (Jakubik 2016b). The practice of protection is an essential mentoring practice that creates a safety net for career development within a supportive mentoring environment.

Effective Mentoring

To mentor effectively, follow the advice and suggestions for best practices in mentoring found here and in other publications. Suggestions include sharing experiences through stories to highlight lessons learned throughout your career. It is better to try to understand the issue before diagnosing or suggesting solutions or advice to solve the problem. The mentor should give the mentee undivided attention and connect with them to ensure they feel heard. Celebrate the mentee's successes and focus on the growth that you have seen in them (Reeves 2022). Empathize with your mentee's challenges and daily struggles. Reassure them that this too will pass, and years from now, they will see this as a unique challenge that strengthened their resolve and enhanced their professional knowledgebase.

Tips for Mentors

Mentors serve as role models and provide guidance and advice to help the mentee grow professionally and personally. What follows are several suggestions for a successful mentorship from the Harvard School of Public Health Career Services:

- Help the mentee set educational/career goals.
- Share information about your background, skills, and interests.
- Encourage open communication and listen actively.
- Celebrate the mentee's milestones and achievements.
- Offer constructive and meaningful advice and feedback.
- Serve as a resource for career information.
- Educate the mentee on workplace expectations. (HSPH 2016)

Tips for Mentees

Mentees serve as observers and learners, responsible for accepting guidance and advice to foster professional and personal growth. What follows are tips for mentees from the International Mentoring Group (https://mentoringgroup.com/).

- Ask for specific advice on leadership and strategy. Be receptive to receiving other perspectives.
- Evaluate advice and feedback to ensure it will work for you.
- Evaluate the relationship to ensure you are getting what you need.
- Be actively committed and take responsibility for the outcome.
- Remember relationships are dynamic and can change at any moment.
- Do not dismiss the value of your peers in the mentoring process. Often, they have valuable information, and they are willing to share.

Incorporating Practical Tips

Mentors

People come from diverse backgrounds and experiences and will receive mentoring differently. Get to know your mentee individually, as this will let you help them set realistic expectations. Scheduling can become challenging when it is necessary to work around business or personal travel. Communicate your availability and make rescheduling a priority. Be responsive to your e-mails, text, and phone calls. Be available to provide advice, guidance, and ask and answer questions using resources, both print and non-print. Encourage open communication and participation by listening actively to ensure you understand what the mentee needs. Consistency is the key to trust. Your level of consistency determines your level of trust. Be willing to make modifications to the mentoring relationship as often as needed.

Create a solid plan of action using educational and career goals as the guide. As you define expectations, set up a system to measure achievement. Recognize the mentee's work and the milestones they have reached. Take the time to celebrate successes and reward milestones. Be truthful in your evaluations but tactful with your feedback delivery. Do not forget to engage in your own learning while you are mentoring. Never miss the opportunity to collaborate on projects, ask questions, discover, experiment, and have fun. Share your ideas, give advice, and be a resource for new innovations. Encourage professional development and participation in local and national professional associations. Serve as an advisor on library and institutional politics. Teach them how to think strategically and make decisions using critical analysis.

Mentees

Mentees must want to learn, grow, and develop new skills to address the challenges and rich opportunities revealed throughout the relationship. Be respectful of your mentor's time, and always show gratitude for their willingness to share their experiences with you. Always keep communication lines open. Do not let your e-mails, text, or voicemail go unanswered. Be upfront about your expectations. Let your mentor know what goals you have set for yourself and what lessons you anticipate gaining from the relationship. Remember that your mentor is there for you but only as a guide. Review your goals often so that you can clearly articulate them to your mentor. This way they know exactly what to expect from you. Let your mentor know if you do not understand something or have a differing opinion. Participate by listening actively and asking questions. Take advantage of opportunities to observe your mentor in practice if he/she is local. Do not hesitate to offer ideas on what activities and exercises you can do together. Be willing to share the latest trends, innovations, and creative techniques that you have been exposed to, with your mentor. Mentors can help you break down silos to foster collaboration. They also can help you realign your thinking, introducing you to additional resources and colleagues with complementary expertise to enhance your knowledge and encourage faster skills development.

Reliability and consistency are necessary for both the mentor and the mentee. Trust is difficult to earn but easily lost. Stay positive as you develop your mentor/mentee relationship. Do not forget that your mentor is offering feedback, not criticism. Prioritize your mentoring relationship by showing your mentor just how important this relationship is. Be willing to make modifications to the mentoring relationship when needed.

Challenges of Mentoring

When starting a mentor/mentee relationship, the mentor must assess the mentee's background to evaluate the level of knowledge and skills they possess and determine what areas of mentorship are needed. A big part of the assessment is identifying the mentee's motivation and career goals.

Often day-to-day activities impede the ability to keep the mentee engaged. Mentors may encounter issues dealing with a mentee's inexperience or a lack of knowledge and skills. Deciding on the best solution to a given mentoring situation can be a challenge, as you always want to give advice that will be beneficial to the mentee in their specific situation. Setting limits and boundaries is necessary for the mentor/mentee relationship to address any misconceptions about the span or depth of mentoring activities. Mentors may struggle with finding ways to build a mentee's confidence or address their lack of planning or lack of progress. It takes time to build relationships. Amid building relationships, mentors often learn from their mentees.

If the mentoring relationship becomes constrained or unhealthy for either party, openly discuss the discontent. This is a crucial conversation. If concerns cannot be resolved, consider discontinuing the agreement. For formal programs, the pair may be matched by program planners and required to stay for the duration of the assignment. For informal matches, mentees should think outside the box before choosing a mentor, and they should be open to diverse individuals. It is essential to create personal networks, so reach out to those you consider worthy. Look for mentoring possibilities inside and outside of librarianship and be strategic about taking advantage of mentoring programs offered through your institution or professional associations.

Other challenges include mentors who are not fully committed and allow their career limitations to cloud their judgment and give jaded advice. If a mentee is interested in obtaining a goal that is not your forte, connect them with a colleague who is more expert on the subject for that aspect of their training and growth. For the continuity of the profession, mentoring must be connected to components that transform librarianship and provide continuous development for librarians at all stages of their careers. Successful mentoring can influence health sciences librarians to become change agents and pave the way for making a difference in how the profession is viewed.

Finding a Mentor

It is important and beneficial for solo and new librarians to find mentors who will help them build essential skills and gain insight into the profession. Hospital librarians may want to explore finding mentors in clinical settings and not necessarily from within librarianship. The right mentor will provide the guidance and support required. Bartley et al. (2021) offer several tips to help new librarians and suggest that finding a mentor is a key to success:

1. Network: Attend library events and conferences. Join professional organizations—not only MLA but also local business or civic organizations. Reach out to people in your network and ask colleagues to see if there is someone willing to take you under their wing.
2. Research: Look for people who are doing things that you would like to do in your career. Once you have identified potential mentors, do your research to get a better understanding of their experience and skills and see what they have accomplished and what they offer you.
3. Reach out: When you are ready, reach out to your potential mentor and start a conversation. Explain why you're interested in working with them, what you hope to gain from the experience, and how you can use their guidance to move ahead in your career.
4. Start informally: Start with finding opportunities to share and ask questions. Find ways to work within your mentor's schedule so that they can easily find time to share with you (Bartley, Simuel, and Williams 2021).

Diversity and Inclusion in Mentoring

Mentorship is critical to recruiting and retaining diverse individuals in the health sciences library profession. It is essential that library leaders be committed to incorporating diversity and inclusion into the workforce. Gender identity, age, ethnicity, and accessibility differences must be considered. It is advantageous for leaders to be willing to mentor demographically and socially different mentees. Mentors must demonstrate their commitment to diversity, equity, inclusion, and belonging (DEIB) by deliberately mentoring people who are different from themselves (Farnell 2017). Leaders tend to coach and mentor "their own," and here's the human impulse that drives it: People naturally invest in and advocate for the development of the subordinates who are most like them. Even those who believe that diversity improves creativity, problem-solving, and decision-making gravitate to those who display similarities. By doing so, they risk cultivating the talents of a homogenous few rather than a distinguishable myriad of potential game changers.

Librarians must overcome the tendency to allow negative stereotypes, biases, or micro-aggressions to get in the way of selecting mentoring participants that vary by gender, race, ethnicity, gender identity, geography, culture, accessibility, expertise, or any number of variables. When leaders commit to mentoring those who are not like themselves, other leaders will join and commit to coaching, advocating, and investing in diverse talent.

On the other hand, connecting Black, Indigenous, and People of Color (BIPOC) with others of similar racial or ethnic groups can be a good strategy at times because these mentors can help mentees maneuver the cultural and political climate of the organization, as well as provide a variety of perspectives. Organizations are missing opportunities to achieve successes by not bringing diversity to their leadership teams (Turner-Moffatt 2019). People of color who advance the farthest all share one characteristic—a strong network of mentors and corporate sponsors who nurture their professional development (Thomas 2001).

Common Goals of Mentoring Programs

The goal of a mentorship program is to accelerate the personal and professional development of mentees (Reeves 2022). Yet, depending on the library's needs, the reasons for having a mentoring program may differ. Table 7.1 illustrates common reasons for beginning mentoring programs and provides suggestions on the type of mentoring to utilize to accomplish each goal.

Table 7.1. Types of Mentoring

Common Mentoring Goals	Optimal Mentoring Program Structure	Optimal Use of Mentoring Types
Develop emerging leaders	Formal	1-on-1 / Collaborative-Group / Team
Reinforce employee training	Formal	Collaborative-Group / Team / Peer / Flash
Induction and onboarding employees faster	Informal	1-on-1 / Peer / Reverse / Flash
Promote diversity, equity & inclusion	Formal or Informal	1-on-1 / Collaborative-Group / Team / Peer / Reverse / Flash
Support employee career development	Formal or Informal	1-on-1 / Collaborative-Group
Foster connections with employees in remote workplaces	Formal or Informal	1-on-1 / Collaborative-Group / Team / Peer / Flash
Aid succession planning	Formal	1-on-1 / Flash / Reverse
Develop high potential employees	Formal	1-on-1 / Collaborative-Group / Team / Peer / Flash
Improve company culture	Formal or Informal	1-on-1 / Collaborative-Group / Team / Reverse
Increase employee retention	Formal	1-on-1 / Collaborative-Group / Team / Reverse
Support employer brand as nurturing organization	Formal or Informal	Collaborative-Group / Team / Peer
Leadership development	Formal	1-on-1 / Collaborative-Group / Team
Promoting women in leadership	Formal	1-on-1 / Collaborative-Group / Team / Reverse
Knowledge retention	Formal or Informal	Collaborative-Group / Team / Flash
Skill sharing	Formal or Informal	Collaborative-Group / Team / Flash / Peer

Source: Adapted from Reeves (2022) and used with permission of the author.

How to Build a Successful Mentoring Program

Mentoring programs will establish specific goals, and both mentors and mentees will benefit from the process by following basic guidelines. Maureen Metcalf (2019), CEO of the Innovative Leadership Institute (https://www.innovativeleadershipinstitute.com/), suggests the following criteria for building a successful mentoring program:

Match people effectively. A critical factor in mentoring success involves matching people correctly to enhance engagement. Many programs create a mentor pool by accepting resumes from potential mentors. Mentees often submit applications and resumes. It is good practice to allow the mentor and the mentees to review applications that align with their skill sets. Effective matching should be based on personality traits, values, work style, and other characteristics, as well as skills and expertise. The matching process intentionally allows for diversity and inclusion by matching men with women and minority mentees with majority mentors. Do not allow unconscious bias to become a barrier to entry for minority mentees.

Commit to the process. Mentoring is more effective when both parties acknowledge that mentoring is an important structural part of the task. The level of commitment to the program needs to be continuously evaluated. Here are several questions that will help with the evaluation and tracking of actual progress in building accountability.

1. How often are mentoring sessions scheduled?
2. Are employees provided with time to mentor or be mentored, or are they expected to work additional hours to make up for mentoring time?
3. How often are mentoring appointments canceled or rescheduled?
4. How often has technology been used as the method of connection?
5. What mentoring activities have enhanced your engagement?

Develop mentoring goals. Each participant in a mentoring program will have different objectives and expectations. It is important for the mentor and mentee to understand their unique objectives and keep them in mind when they structure their individual mentoring plan and their mentoring sessions. Mentors and mentees should revisit goals to course correct and ensure the desired outcomes on a pre-set basis.

Provide process support tools. Mentors and mentees may want to incorporate tools to support their process. Tools can take the form of step-by-step guides, process recommendations, or internal business processes used to provide structure. Delivery methods can include one-on-one sharing sessions, online resources, books or workbooks, videos, podcasts, or other learning environments.

Commit to regular contact. Consistency is important to building a strong relationship and accomplishing goals. Commit to a regular schedule and honor that commitment like you honor other commitments you value. How often you meet will be influenced by factors such as mentoring goals, workload, program structure, and organizational culture.

Track goals. It is important to track your goal attainment and correct your course when necessary. It is useful to set a pre-determined frequency to review goals, the mentoring process, and your feelings about the relationship. Strategies for tracking include breaking up goals into incremental tasks, assigning manageable deadlines, reviewing progress, adjusting regularly, and making goal-tracking a collaborative activity.

Close the mentoring relationship. Mentors and mentees will, at some point, transition out of a formal mentoring arrangement. Acknowledging the investment that the mentor and mentee have made to the mentoring process is the first step toward closure. Many formal mentoring relationships evolve into informal relationships when participants align their schedules and decide how to stay in touch after the formal mentoring relationship ends.

Develop a culture of mentorship. Mentorship must be a team effort, but the team starts from the top. You must get the C-suite onboard. Eliminate silos and encourage collaboration throughout your organization. Pair mentors and mentees with complementary skills and consider pairs to facilitate addressing the development of new skills. Make mentoring accessible to all employees by embracing inclusivity. Structure your program for maximum accountability and measured outcomes. Start mentoring activities from the date employees are hired by incorporating mentoring activities. Encourage mentees to show initiative and step up to lead projects and new initiatives. Keep your focus on communication, a critical element for the success of the mentoring relationship. Utilize the teachable moments for circular mentoring for all employees. To strengthen mentoring in your organization, learning and growth must be embedded in your culture.

Conclusion

Mentoring is critical for growing future leaders, and each of us is responsible for providing the guidance and inspiration to give new health sciences librarians and staff the knowledge and tools to thrive in their careers. Positive prior mentoring experiences lay a critical foundation for mentoring that can facilitate opportunities for engagement in scholarly activities. Your path to leadership success in the immediate future will be positively impacted by effective mentoring. Mentors who have been well mentored tend to become great mentors themselves and are able to assess what mentees are thinking and, in turn, gain insight about the person and the organization (Maggart and James 1999). Mentorship is imperative to the success of every library; it should, therefore, be elevated to the level of a major priority. Successful mentoring nurtures mentees who eventually develop into leaders and become mentors themselves.

Kouzes and Posner (https://www.leadershipchallenge.com/research/five-practices.aspx) identified five exemplary practices that consistently enable leaders to achieve extraordinary results:

- **Model the way**: Leaders set examples for others by consistently aligning their actions and values.
- **Inspire a shared vision**: Leaders inspire a shared vision by exciting and energizing others. They hold out a vision of the possible.
- **Challenge the process**: Leaders step out into the unknown and search for opportunities. They innovate, experiment, take risks, and welcome innovative ideas.
- **Enable others to act**: By leading "through" others, leaders strengthen their peers and form strong collaborative relationships.
- **Encourage the heart**: In these stressful and uncertain times, encouraging the heart is especially important to both achieving results and maintaining relationships.

These practices provide a coherent framework for mentoring future leaders and are also essential competencies for leaders themselves (Zachary 2010).

Select Mentor and Mentee Opportunities

Both authors have participated in formal and informal mentoring programs. Select programs include the following:

AAMLA (African American Medical Librarians Alliance/MLA) Mentoring Program: AAMLA members informally mentor members of this MLA caucus on leadership, providing guidance and support.
ARL (Association of Research Libraries) Leadership and Career Development Fellows: The ARL leadership program is a yearlong fellowship. It is focused on preparing mid-career librarians from historically underrepresented racial and ethnic groups to assume leadership roles in their careers and in the profession at large.

- **Minnesota Institute (The Minnesota Institute for Early Career Librarians from Traditionally Underrepresented Groups)**: The Institute's goal is to develop leadership skills in library leaders from diverse backgrounds. Participants enhance self-awareness and leadership skills to transform and create more equitable work environments.
- **MLA (Medical Library Association) Mentoring Program**: MLA provides members with the opportunity to serve as a mentor or to request a mentor. Those who participate in the AHIP (Academy of Health Information Professionals) Credentialing Program will be paired with another AHIP member to help guide them through the program.
- **MLA Rising Star Program**: The MLA Rising Star Program gives members the opportunity to develop skills, knowledge, and personal characteristics needed to become MLA leaders. The yearly leadership development program matches each Rising Star with a mentor and provides opportunities to gain a comprehensive, intimate view of all aspects of MLA, from board meetings to MLA history, with a focus on strategic planning.
- **NLM/AAHSL (National Library of Medicine/Association of Academic Health Sciences Libraries) Leadership Fellows Program**: The NLM/AAHSL Leadership Fellows Program identifies emerging leaders in health sciences libraries who desire to gain leadership skills and knowledge to lead academic health sciences libraries in the future.
- **VA (Department of Veterans Affairs) Mentorship Program**: Newly appointed VA library managers participate in a mentor program that pairs each one with an experienced VA librarian to orient them to VA leadership and management practices.

Discussion Questions

1. What are three important characteristics/qualities you prefer in an individual that you think will be best suited to meet your mentoring needs?
2. As a mentor, do I have the skills, time, and sufficient professional networks of colleagues to successfully mentor?
3. As a mentee, have I defined my expectations, and am I willing to commit the time and resources to learn and grow professionally and personally?

Acknowledgement

Sincere appreciation to Rosalind K. Lett for her contributions in editing, reviewing content, and adapting Table 7.1 for this chapter.

Suggested Readings

Abolarinwa, Shola Timothy, and Japheth Abdulazeez Yaya. 2016. "The Place of Mentoring in Developing Librarians' Leadership Competency." *Asian Journal of Education and e-Learning* 4, no. 1: 7–14.

Alston, Geleana D., and Catherine A. Hansman. 2020. "Embracing Diversity and Inclusive Mentoring Practices for Leadership Development." *New Directions for Adult & Continuing Education* (167/168): 83–94. doi: 10.1002/ace.20400.

Bunnett, Brian, Nancy Allee, Jo Dorsch, Gabriel Rios, and Cindy Stewart. 2009. "Embracing Diversity and Inclusive Mentoring Practices for Leadership Development (NLM/AAHSL) Leadership Fellows Program: A Year in Review." *Journal of Library Administration* 49, no. 8: 869–79.

Couture, Juliann, Jennie Gerke, and Jennifer Knievel. 2020. "Getting Into the Club: Existence and Availability of Mentoring for Tenured Librarians in Academic Libraries." *College & Research Libraries* 81, no. 4: 1–33.

Farmer, Diana, Marcia G. Stockham, and Alice Trussell. 2009. "Revitalizing a Mentoring Program for Academic Librarians." *College & Research Libraries* 7, no. 1: 8–24.

Johnson, Peggy. 2007. "Retaining and Advancing Librarians of Color." *College & Research Libraries* 68, no. 5: 405–17.

Jones, Shannon D., and Beverly Murphy. 2019. *Diversity and Inclusion in Libraries: A Call to Action and Strategies for Success*: Lanham, MD: Rowman & Littlefield.

Laynor, Gregory, and Natalie Tagge. 2022. "Developing Pathways to Health Sciences Librarianship with an Introductory Course and Mentoring Program." *The Reference Librarian* 63, no. 3: 67–81.

Lee, Yejin. 2020. "Mentorship as a Tool for Growth, Inclusion, and Equity." www.idealist.org/en/careers/mentorship-diversity-inclusion.

Leuzinger, Julie Ann, and Jennifer Rowe. 2017. "Succession Planning Through Mentoring in the Library." *Library Leadership & Management* 31, no. 4.

Marshall, Caroline, and Helen-Ann Brown Epstein. 2021. "So You Want to Be a Hospital Librarian: Pathways to Get There." *Journal of Hospital Librarianship* 21, no. 1: 67–71.

References

Bartley, Kelsa, Jahala Simuel, and Jamia Williams. 2021. "New to Health Sciences Librarianship: Strategies, Tips, and Tricks." *Journal of the Medical Library Association : JMLA* 109, no. 2: 330–35. doi: 10.5195/jmla.2021.1184.

Bynum, Yvette P. 2015. "The Power of Informal Mentoring." *Education* 136, no. 1: 69–73.

Cambridge Dictionary. "Mentor." Accessed March 23, 2022. https://dictionary.cambridge.org/us/dictionary/english/mentor.

Eden, Bradford. 2017. "What It Means to be a Leader in Academic Libraries in the Twenty-first Century." In Carl Antonucci and Sharon Clapp, eds. *The LITA Leadership Guide: The Librarian as Entrepreneur, Leader, and Technologist*, 11. Lanham, MD: Rowman & Littlefield.

Farnell, Richard. 2017. "Mentor People Who Aren't Like You." *Harvard Business Review*. https://hbr.org/2017/04/mentor-people-who-arent-like-you.

Harvard School of Public Health – Career Services (HSPH). 2015. "The Mentor–Mentee Relationship." https://cdn1.sph.harvard.edu/wp-content/uploads/sites/36/2016/06/The-Mentor-Mentee-Relationship-Handout_October-2015.pdf.

Jakubik, Louise D., Aris B. Eliades, Meghan M. Weese, and Jennifer J. Huth. 2016a. "Mentoring Practice and Mentoring Benefit 2: Mapping the Future and Career Optimism—An Overview and Application to Practice Using Mentoring Activities." *Pediatric Nursing* 42, no. 3: 145–46.

———. 2016b. "Mentoring Practice and Mentoring Benefit 5: Providing Protection and Security—An Overview and Application to Practice Using Mentoring Activities." *Pediatric Nursing* 42, no. 6: 300–1.

Kouzes, James M., and Barry Posner. "This is What it Means to Lead: Five Practices of Exemplary Leadership Model." Accessed November 11, 2022. https://www.leadershipchallenge.com/research/five-practices.aspx.

Maggart, Lon E., and Jeanette S. James. 1999. "Mentoring—A Critical Element in Leader Development." *Military Review* 79, no. 3: 86–87.

Metcalf, Maureen. 2019. "Seven Keys to Creating a High-Impact Mentoring Program." https://www.forbes.com/sites/forbescoachescouncil/2019/10/23/seven-keys-to-creating-a-high-impact-mentoring-program/?sh=16d7dd636acb.

Metros, Susan E., and Catherine Yang. 2006. "Chapter 5: The Importance of Mentors." The Ohio State University. Accessed November 9, 2022. https://www.educause.edu/research-and-publications/books/cultivating-careers-professional-development-campus-it/chapter-5-importance-mentors.

Reeves, Matthew. 2022. "Objectives and Goals for Your Workplace Mentoring Program," *Together* (blog). February 18, 2022. https://www.togetherplatform.com/blog/objectives-and-goals-for-your-workplace-mentoring-program.

Schumer, Lizz. 2018. "Why Mentoring Matters and How to Get Started," *New York Times*, September 26, 2018. https://www.nytimes.com/2018/09/26/smarter-living/why-mentoring-matters-how-to-get-started.html.

Shea, Gordon F. 1994. *Mentoring: Helping Employees Reach Their Full Potential*. New York: American Management Association.

Srivastava, Sameer B. 2015. "Network Intervention: Assessing the Effects of Formal Mentoring on Workplace Networks." *Social Forces* 94, no. 1: 427–52. doi: 10.1093/sf/sov041.

Thomas, David A. 2001. "The Truth about Mentoring Minorities. Race Matters." *Harvard Business Review* 79, no. 4: 98–107, 168.

Turner-Moffatt, Crystal. 2019. "The Power of Mentorship: Strengthening Women in Leadership Roles." *Professional Safety* 64, no. 8: 17–19.

Vital, Fernanda, and Helena Alves. 2010. "The Importance of Welcoming New Health Care Employees and its Impact on Work Motivation and Satisfaction." *Asia Pacific Journal of Business and Management* 1, no. 1: 15–28.

Zachary, Lois J., and Lory A. Fischler. 2010. "Those Who Lead, Mentor." *T+D* 64, no. 3: 52–57.

8

Path to Leadership

Rick L. Fought

Key Points

We examined the career journey of academic health sciences library directors to better understand their leadership development and what led them to their leadership positions in libraries.

A qualitative phenomenological approach was employed due to its focus on exploring and understanding the meaning individuals ascribe to a particular phenomenon or experience. Eleven library directors from academic health sciences libraries at public universities with very high research activity agreed to participate in the study. The research question guiding this study was: What was the library directors' career journey that led them into library leadership?

A major theme that emerged from the data was "Path to Leadership." Although each participant's journey was unique, there were common elements that surfaced as they chronicled their careers that were informative to how they understood their emergence and development as library leaders. The four categories defining the theme were "Breadth of Experience," "Focused Preparation," "Mentors," and "Recognizing/Developing Leadership Potential."

Previous research suggests that leadership development and preparedness are important contributors to leadership effectiveness. It was encouraging to witness and understand the amount of preparation by participants to ready themselves for their roles as library directors. This chapter provides a comprehensive view of the path to library leadership that furthers our understanding of the value of leadership development and preparedness and provides a model for aspiring library leaders.

Introduction

Leadership development and preparedness are important contributors to leadership effectiveness (Weiner 2003). Several studies have examined the leadership development of academic library directors and have evaluated how the library profession has promoted leadership development (Bonnette 2004; Feldmann et al. 2013; Fitsimmons 2008; Lipscomb, Martin, and Peay 2009; Parch and Baughman 2010; Rooney 2010; Skinner and Krabbenhoeft 2014). Most of this research has focused on mentoring, on-the-job training, library leadership training programs, and leadership development and preparedness in general. Lipscomb et al. (2009), for example, studied the National Library of Medicine/Association of Academic Health Sciences Libraries (NLM/AAHSL) Leadership Fellows Program and found that study participants believed the program helped individuals in their leadership development, contributed to the quality of leadership in the library profession, and improved succession planning and leadership development for AAHSL. A few other studies focused on specific topics such as the necessity and value of a doctorate degree among small college library directors (McCracken 2000).

Each study has proved useful for understanding why leadership development and preparedness is important and what leadership skills a person should develop to prepare for a leadership position. Unfortunately, no library studies have provided a full picture allowing readers to understand how various elements of leadership development and preparedness interrelate and progress during one's career journey. A cohesive picture of this career journey into library leadership would further our understanding of the value of leadership development and preparedness and could serve as a model for those interested in moving into leadership positions at their libraries.

We specifically wanted to better understand the career journey of a library director at an academic health sciences library through an examination of the research participants' experiences. We focused expressly on exploring the path and decisions that led them to leadership positions and how they prepared themselves to be effective leaders.

Methods

A qualitative phenomenological approach was employed in this study due to its emphasis on analyzing and understanding the personal experiences of academic health sciences library directors. The study concentrated on their perceptions and understanding of their leadership development and preparedness during their career journey toward becoming library directors. Qualitative phenomenological research was an appropriate design due to its focus on exploring and understanding the meaning individuals ascribe to a particular phenomenon or experience (Merriam and Tisdell 2015). Phenomenology attempts to get to the essence of a shared experience and works particularly well when studying phenomena that are difficult to quantify, such as leadership (Käufer and Chemero 2015).

Study participants were selected using a purposeful sampling process coupled with criterion-based sampling strategies. Purposeful sampling targets highly selective, information-rich cases or participants that are better able to explain and clarify the research questions (Patton 2014). For this study, the most appropriate participants were determined to be academic health sciences library directors. Criterion-based sampling strategies use predetermined criteria to eliminate participants who do not meet the criteria (Patton 2014). Participants met the following predetermined criteria: they were directors, or had equivalent titles, at public universities classified as RU/VH (research university/very high research activity), according to the US Carnegie Classification of Institutions of Higher Education. Health sciences libraries at these institutions are typically larger, have more employees, and potentially work with a broader and more complex range of issues than directors at smaller institutions, which could yield a richer and more complete understanding of leadership at academic health sciences libraries. Additionally, the list of participants also met the criterion of active AAHSL membership. An initial scan of universities meeting these criteria identified forty-eight institutions. A purposeful sampling of fifteen academic health sciences library directors at these institutions were invited to participate in the study. These fifteen institutions were selected primarily due to their geographic location to ensure all areas of the United States were included. Eleven participants accepted the invitation.

There is no exact determination of the number of participants that is adequate, as the intent of qualitative research is not to generalize the information but to explain participants' specific personal experiences (Meriam and Tisdell 2015; Glesne 2016). However, Seidman recommends using two criteria to determine when a research study has a sufficient number of participants (Seidman 2013). The first criterion is sufficiency: Are there enough participants in the study so that individuals outside the sample group can connect to the experience of those who are in it? There must be a sufficient number of participants to reflect the wide range of individuals and contexts found in academic health science centers. The second criterion is saturation of information: Does the researcher reach a point where he or she hears the same information from participants and no new information is being conveyed? At some point, a researcher no longer learns anything new, and at that point, any further data collection may be of limited value, although it is difficult to predetermine when this might occur (Seidman 2013). Seidman, therefore, does not recommend a specific number of participants, as every researcher and every study is different, but they do mention practical exigencies of time, money, and other resources as also playing roles in determining the number of participants in a study (Seidman 2013). We believe that both of Seidman's criteria were met in regard to the number of participants in this study. Approval from the governing institutional review board was granted prior to contact with the participants in this study.

Data were collected primarily through phenomenological, semi-structured interviews. Two interviews were done with each participant, which allowed them time to "reconstruct and reflect upon their experience within the context of their lives" (Seidman 2013). The interviews used primarily open-ended questions structured around the research question but allowed new ideas to be brought into the interviews based on how participants responded. All interviews were conducted over the phone and were recorded to ensure accuracy and completeness. The interviews were later transcribed in preparation for coding.

Interview data were transcribed and analyzed using thematic analysis. Thematic analysis segregates data into groups with the use of codes or labels and searches for patterns that can be organized into broader categories. These categories are then constructed into themes that represent meaning from the data in response to the research questions (Meriam and Tisdell 2015; Glesne 2016). The order or combination of themes and categories for this study was dictated by the data. During analysis, there were certain ideas and perceptions that stood out more than others, and their prominence was important to understanding the essence of this shared experience in leadership.

Qualitative research uses different standards of rigor than quantitative research to ensure trustworthiness. To a certain extent, the trustworthiness of a qualitative study is dependent on a thorough and rigorous research design (Merriam and Tisdell 2015). This study also used member checking, peer debriefing, and triangulation to ensure its trustworthiness. Member checking is where the researcher gives participants the opportunity to explain any of their interview answers and comment on whether their interview accurately and fully reflects their experience of the phenomenon under study (Creswell and Poth 2013). Peer debriefing is an external review of the research process done for the researcher by a peer who provides an independent viewpoint (Creswell and Poth 2013). Finally, triangulation refers to the use of multiple data collection methods and/or multiple data sources to substantiate the research findings (Meriam and Tisdell 2015; Glesne 2016). Subjectivity or bias is unavoidable when conducting research. It is incumbent on researchers to acknowledge this and to attempt to identify their subjectivities, assumptions, and stereotypes throughout the course of their research (Glesne 2016). Although acknowledgment of this subjectivity or bias does not eliminate it, it allows researchers to manage and minimize their impact on the research process and achieve a better understanding of themselves (Glesne 2016). In this study, one researcher is an experienced librarian in a leadership position at an academic health sciences library, and the other is a professor of education with no prior work in libraries. Both are very interested in the study of leadership effectiveness in higher education.

Results

After analyzing the data gathered from this research question, we determined that one major theme emerged, with four categories defining the theme. The theme was labeled "Path to Leadership" and its four categories were Breadth of Experience, Focused Preparation, Mentors, and Recognizing/Developing Leadership Potential. Pseudonyms are used to protect the identities of the research participants.

Breadth of Experience

Several participants communicated during their interviews how the position of library director required a broad perspective and an understanding of the big picture of how academic health sciences libraries work and how they fit in at their institutions—now and in the future. They believed this was critical for a director to be effective and do their job well. As they spoke about their individual paths to their positions of leadership, the variation in the education and work experiences of the participants was remarkable, including one participant with a master's degree in Business Administration and another with a law degree. For instance, Patricia worked a variety of positions before becoming the director, each of which provided her with valuable experience that prepared her well for her future role:

> I have worked across like all areas of the library. I was a cataloger for a year. I worked in technical services for a year. I was an assistant director. I was head of a small library, small two-, three-person library. I dealt in such a wide range of health sciences from medical education to medical research to healthcare policy. I really think that breadth of exposure in those three very different institutions I worked at gave me a broad perspective, an ability to detect, not quite the right word, but to suss what's really critical, what's really good practice, and what's just local custom. And I felt really prepared when I came to [my current position] for the challenge that I was given here.

Another important aspect of this category pertained to opportunities for growth and experience given to participants at various stages of their career that allowed them to develop their leadership skills and learn important lessons regarding how academic health sciences libraries work. For example, Terri spoke about opportunities she was given that she thought were instrumental in her personal leadership development:

> I was given an opportunity to organize a conference for the whole campus. It was going to be a technology expo. I was given stretch assignments and conference event planning exercises. There was another opportunity [at my library] where I had to decommission all photocopiers and move us to a printing card system. I also had to move us from a home-grown system to a commercial-based library integrated system. We went from a home-grown system to Innovative Interfaces, Inc. So, I guess, I was given a lot of implementation assignments. I had to do the research or was part of the team that did the research. But I just remember those being really risky, fun, rewarding opportunities that really challenged me and kept me motivated, and I appreciated the fact that those directors really were willing to take a risk on me.

It was during this time that participants said they started thinking that they could be directors at some point in their future and initiated a more deliberate plan of preparation to help them achieve that goal.

Focused Preparation

Once the goal of becoming an academic health sciences director was set, many participants took a more focused and planned approach to preparing themselves for that position. They had been exposed to enough leadership opportunities that they understood better where they needed to develop their skills and gain more experience. Many participants took advantage of opportunities provided by their universities and/or professional organizations to develop their leadership abilities. Olivia talked about specific leadership skills she sought to develop to provide herself with a solid foundation before becoming director. Specifically, she mentioned leadership classes on hiring employees, budgeting, and interpersonal relationships.

Several specific leadership programs were mentioned by multiple participants as being particularly helpful in their development as leaders. Each participant took something different from the programs, but all of them found the experience valuable and an important step in their path toward becoming a library director. For some, the experience served, among other things, as a confidence booster. One research participant, Karen, had this to say:

> One thing that helped me gain more confidence was getting the opportunity to attend the Bryn Mawr Summer Institute for Women in Higher Education Administration. Those kinds of opportunities I thought were really helpful not only in building skills and perspective, but also providing a little bit of a jolt or booster. Morale booster as well as a knowledge booster. I had also gone to the Harvard/ACRL Leadership Institute for Academic Librarians. While Bryn Mawr was three weeks and a half and residential [chuckles], ACRL was one week and residential. But what was packed into that week was just incredible. I think the thing that I really liked the best about it was learning about the four frames because it helped me get even a quicker way of understanding what's going on around me and how to interpret things. I found that very valuable.

The main program mentioned by participants regarding their leadership development was the NLM/AAHSL Leadership Fellows Program, a year-long intensive leadership program designed to prepare emerging leaders for the position of library director in academic health sciences libraries (Lipscomb, Martin, and Peay 2009). Several research participants had been part of this program and spoke well of its contribution to their development as leaders in academic health sciences libraries. Debra said:

> So basically, doing the AAHSL Leadership Fellow Program, the one-year leadership institute, was really good for me. It helped reframe many things I had been doing and gave them a name and then I understood what it was I had been doing. And going forward I felt more empowered with that knowledge, knowing what I needed to do. And I do a lot of leadership CEs, I read a lot, I have a vast collection of supervisory manuals. I also go to the CEs here at [my university] where they offer a 6-month leadership training class, supervisory training class. [My alma mater] had a supervisory training class that lasted 6 weeks. So, I've been through all the training courses at [my alma mater] and [my university], learning as much as I possibly could and applying as much as I possibly can in the role I currently have.

The research participants dedicated countless hours toward the singular task of developing their leadership abilities to add to their already solid foundation of knowledge and skills regarding libraries in general. Once they decided to take that next step in their career, they understood the need for additional knowledge and experience to be successful and then selectively sought out that knowledge and experience.

Mentors

Another important part of leadership development mentioned by several participants was mentors who helped them at various stages of their careers. Mentor relationships were described by many as being valuable in advancing the participants' careers. Mentors not only educated participants about the demands of leadership at academic health sciences libraries but also served as sounding boards for ideas and advice once the participants began moving into leadership positions. When asked about what made the biggest difference in her development as a leader, Mary Lou replied:

> I think having a boss who acted as a mentor and I was very, very fortunate to have had an excellent boss who was also a very good mentor. She would challenge me to think differently about how I might approach a problem, and she would let me sit in with her on certain leadership opportunities. I think having a boss and a mentor who sees opportunities and then can match those opportunities to who you are as person are very important. And she had a gift to be able to do that. She has not only done that with me, she's done it with several others. And so that really helped to form my experiences as a library director.

Jill and Terri mentioned seeking out mentors who modeled the behaviors they thought were effective and were on the career path they hoped to follow. These mentors were considered to have the types of knowledge, skills, and experiences they were seeking. In turn, these mentors went beyond imparting advice and wisdom and directly helped the participants advance their careers. Terri mentioned, "I had great mentors along the way and some of my mentors were always watching out for me for next career opportunities."

Almost every research participant mentioned a mentoring relationship they had experienced somewhere during their path to becoming a library director. In each case, they spoke about this mentor relationship in reverent terms and expressed a desire to mentor librarians themselves. They deeply appreciated the mentoring they received and wanted to give that same experience back to the next generation of library leaders.

Recognizing/Developing Leadership Potential

The last category for this theme provided a deeper look at how participants recognized and developed their own leadership potential, as well as how they recognize emerging leaders in the library profession and what they do to assist in developing that leadership potential. Richard said the following about what he looks for in potential library leaders:

> I know the big one I looked for, and that was people that could see a big picture. People that didn't focus so narrowly on their own set of duties that they couldn't grasp the way the whole system worked. They had to know their role in our library system in the library here but boy, if you can't see how that fits into a larger picture, you're sort of doomed. And I have seen people tripped up by that, who just won't pull back and see the bigger picture. Now, how I know if they're seeing the bigger picture or not, I don't know. I guess what the things they're interested in, what kind of projects they take on, even the way they develop relationships with other faculty within the library and within our constituent groups, I guess. So, I guess that's what I'm looking for, the way they build relationships and the way they sort of build their worldview.

Several participants mentioned being enthusiastic, having a good attitude, and being able to move things forward as good signs of leadership potential. Lily described people with leadership potential as overachievers who always tried to exceed expectations. Dean made similar comments regarding initiative and high expectations. It was clear from the interviews that many directors wanted people who had the stamina, energy, and passion to perform at what experience had told them was a highly demanding position that has a tremendous impact on its institution.

In terms of how these directors helped someone they thought showed leadership potential, many participants would give them projects as opportunities to develop their leadership potential. Hannah spoke of giving her staff increasingly large projects as they proved themselves capable of handling the work and responsibility. She described her process like this:

> I give people smaller projects and see how they do, and then give them bigger projects and watch them succeed. And I keep an eye on them and not just throw them in the deep end, but try to coach them in how to succeed, I think. People that can listen benefit from the coaching. Some people, you can tell them, but they just don't get it. So, people who have good judgment and a good attitude, you can teach them what they need to know in terms of skills.

Each participant seemed especially excited to talk about their efforts to help, encourage, and develop new leaders in academic health sciences libraries. In discussions with participants about their experiences along the career path that led them to becoming library directors, it was clear that they did not do it alone. They benefited greatly from mentors, leadership development programs offered by library professional organizations, and many opportunities given by supervisors over the course of their careers. In this spirit, they were eager to do the same for others and seemed to enjoy passing on the lessons they learned along their journey perhaps more than any other part of their experience as library directors.

Discussion

We sought to better understand the career journey of a library director at an academic health sciences library through an examination of research participants' experiences. Specifically, we were interested in the preparation and path that led participants to the leadership positions they currently held at their libraries. Our findings are consistent with most other research on leadership development in academic libraries. However, whereas previous studies concentrated mostly on a particular aspect of leadership development, such as the most desirable traits for library directors or mentorship, we examined the larger process of preparing to become a library director (Mavrinac 2005; Young, Hernon, and Powell 2006). For example, all directors in the study mentioned their prior library experience, specific leadership training programs, and/or mentor relationships as being critical to their preparedness as library directors. The participants also mentioned being active in several professional library organizations. This supports the findings of O'Keeffe's survey showing that directors prepared themselves for the position through education attainment, prior experience, and professional activities (O'Keeffe, Willinsky, and Maggio 2011). O'Keeffe, however, did not address mentors or how these directors recognized and developed their leadership potential.

Most research participants spoke directly about mentoring relationships they had throughout their careers that were beneficial to them. Kirkland and Bonnette studied the benefits of mentors to women and minorities, respectively, in attaining leadership positions in academic libraries, while Mavrinac made a case for peer mentoring to foster leadership development (Bonnette 2004; Mavrinac 2005; Kirkland 1997). Together, the present and previous studies suggest that mentoring is valuable to leadership development and produces positive outcomes. Several of our research participants expressed a desire to serve as mentors for potential new library leaders, illustrating the value of these relationships.

Many of our research participants were involved with the NLM/AAHSL Leadership Fellows Program. As previously mentioned, this is a one-year program designed to prepare emerging leaders for the position of library director in academic health sciences libraries (Lipscomb, Martin, and Peay 2009). Debra mentioned her experience with the program as being one of the most useful activities for preparing herself to become a library director. Terri and Lily both discussed how important going through the program was for their careers and that it was a capstone experience that brought many academic health sciences library leadership concepts together for them. When Lipscomb et al. reviewed the program by interviewing past fellow graduates (Lipscomb, Martin, and Peay 2009), they found that the program enhanced leadership skills, provided fellows with a network of peers, and gave them credibility as candidates for library director positions. Discussions with research participants who took part in the program confirmed these findings.

The implications of this study are significant for librarians considering a move into leadership positions. While every research participant's journey to leadership was unique, there were common themes that emerged that can serve as a model or guide for someone thinking about becoming a library director, particularly in an academic health sciences library. For librarians already in leadership positions, this study could better enable them to identify those people with leadership potential and give them a guide as to how to develop that potential. As libraries currently face challenging times, developing effective leadership is important to our future success (Fought and Misawa 2018).

There are notable limitations of this study that bear mentioning. Data collection, including the two phenomenologically based, semi-structured interviews, and completing the transcription and analysis of the data, was completed in approximately three months. The second interview with each participant was conducted approximately one week after the first interview. Although this three-month period for data collection and analysis was adequate, we would have benefited from more time for analysis. It would have been better to have scheduled visits to all of the participants' libraries. Also, the interviews typically lasted between thirty to sixty minutes, and more depth and detail could have been gained by extending the interviews to sixty to ninety minutes, if the participants' schedules allowed.

Future research in this area could expand to investigating new library directors, better understanding the challenges they face and how well they are meeting those challenges. As important as it is to support and develop librarians aspiring to become leaders, it is equally important to continue encouraging and developing their leadership potential after they become library directors. Also, there continues to be a need to sufficiently measure library directors' effectiveness (Fagan 2012). Finally, it would be interesting to explore whether or how the experiences of academic health sciences library directors might differ from traditional academic or hospital library directors.

In summary, we sought to better understand the career journey of library directors at academic health sciences libraries and how they prepared themselves to be effective leaders. We identified a theme from the data—Path to Leadership—with four categories that distilled the essence of the participants' experiences as they developed and prepared themselves for effective leadership. These four categories—Breadth of Experience, Focused Preparation, Mentors, and Recognizing/Developing Leadership Potential—can serve as guides for librarians who are considering leadership positions in their careers and for current library directors who are interested in identifying and developing librarians with leadership potential. The study also provides a comprehensive view of the path to library leadership that furthers our understanding of the value of leadership development and preparedness.

This chapter was originally published in the *Journal of the Medical Library Association*.

Discussion Questions

1. How could health sciences libraries better identify librarians with leadership potential?
2. What are some ways health sciences libraries could foster leadership development earlier in librarians' careers?
3. How do you determine what leadership preparation is needed for you to be an effective library director?

Recommended Reading

Ashiq, M., S. U. Rehman, M. Safdar, and H. Ali. 2021. "Academic Library Leadership in the Dawn of the New Millennium: A Systematic Literature Review." *The Journal of Academic Librarianship* 47, no. 3: 102355. https://doi.org/10.1016/j.acalib.2021.102355.

Harris-Keith, C. S. 2016. "What Academic Library Leadership Lacks: Leadership Skills Directors Are Least Likely to Develop, and Which Positions Offer Development Opportunities." *The Journal of Academic Librarianship* 42, no. 4: 313–18. doi.org/10.1016/j.acalib.2016.06.005.

Johnson, J. I., and P. D. Sobczak. 2021. "Leadership and Leader Development: Perspectives from Museum and Academic Library Professionals." *Curator* 64: 269–95. https://doi.org/10.1111/cura.12409.

Oakleaf, M. 2010. *The Value of Academic Libraries: A Comprehensive Research Review and Report*. Chicago, IL: Association of College and Research Libraries.

Wong, G. K. W. 2017. "Leadership and Leadership Development in Academic Libraries: A Review." *Library Management* 38, no. 2/3: 153–66. https://doi.org/10.1108/LM-09-2016-0075.

References

Bonnette, Ashley E. 2004. "Mentoring Minority Librarians Up the Career Ladder." *Library Leadership & Management* 18, no. 3: 134–39.

Creswell, John W., and Cheryl N. Poth. 2013. *Qualitative Inquiry and Research Design: Choosing Among Five Approaches*. 3rd ed. Los Angeles, CA: SAGE Publications.

Fagan, Jody C. 2012. "The Effectiveness of Academic Library Deans and Directors." *Library Leadership & Management* 26, no. 1: 1–19.

Feldmann, L. M., V. Level, and S. Liu. 2013. "Leadership Training and Development: An Academic Library's Findings." *Library Management* 34, no. 1/2: 99–101. doi: 10.1108/01435121311298306.

Fitsimmons, Gary Neil. 2008. "Academic Library Directors in the Eyes of Hiring Administrators: A Comparison of the Attributes, Qualifications, and Competencies Desired by Chief Academic Officers with Those Recommended by Academic Library Directors." In E. D. Garten, D. E. Williams, J. M. Nyce, and J. Golden, eds. *Advances in Library Administration and Organization.* Vol. 26, pp. 265–315. Bingley, UK: Emerald Group Publishing.

Fought, Rick L., and Mitsunori Misawa. 2018. "Accepting the Challenge: What Academic Health Sciences Library Directors Do to Become Effective Leaders." *Journal of the Medical Library Association: JMLA* 106, no. 2: 219–26. doi: 10.5195/jmla.2018.350.

Glesne, Corrine. 2016. *Becoming Qualitative Researchers: An Introduction.* 4th ed. Boston, MA: Pearson.

Käufer, Stephan, and Anthony Chemero. *Phenomenology: An Introduction.* Malden, MA: Polity Press; 2015.

Kirkland, Janice J. 1997. "The Missing Women Library Directors: Deprivation Versus Mentoring." *College & Research Libraries* 58, no. 4: 375–83. doi: 10.5860/crl.58.4.375.

Lipscomb, Carolyn E., Elaine R. Martin, and Wayne J. Peay. 2009. "Building the Next Generation of Leaders: The NLM/AAHSL Leadership Fellows Program." *Journal of Library Administration* 49, no. 8: 847–67.

Mavrinac, Mary Ann. 2005. "Transformational Leadership: Peer Mentoring as a Values-Based Learning Process." *portal: Libraries and the Academy* 5, no. 3: 391–404. doi: 10.1353/pla.2005.0037.

McCracken, Peter. 2000. "The Presence of the Doctorate Among Small College Library Directors." *College & Research Libraries* 61, no. 5 (2000): 400–8. doi: 10.5860/crl.61.5.400.

Merriam, Sharan B., and Elizabeth J. Tisdell. 2015. *Qualitative Research: A Guide to Design and Implementation.* New York: John Wiley & Sons.

O'Keeffe, Jamie, John Willinsky, and Lauren Maggio. 2011. "Public Access and Use of Health Research: An Exploratory Study of the National Institutes of Health (NIH) Public Access Policy Using Interviews and Surveys of Health Personnel." *Journal of Medical Internet Research* 13, no. 4: e1827.

Parsch, Janet H., and M. Sue Baughman. 2010. "Towards Healthy Organizations: The Use of Organization Development in Academic Libraries." *The Journal of Academic Librarianship* 36, no. 1: 3–19. doi: 10.1016/j.acalib.2009.11.002.

Patton, Michael Quinn. 2014. *Qualitative Research & Evaluation Methods: Integrating Theory and Practice.* Thousand Oaks, CA: SAGE Publications; 2015.

Rooney, Michael P. 2010. "The Current State of Middle Management Preparation, Training, and Development in Academic Libraries." *The Journal of Academic Librarianship* 36, no. 5: 383–93. doi: 10.1016/j.acalib.2010.06.002.

Seidman, Irving. 2013. *Interviewing as Qualitative Research: A Guide for Researchers in Education and the Social Sciences.* 4th ed. New York: Teachers College Press; 2013.

Skinner, Katherine, and Nick Krabbenhoeft. 2014. "Training the 21st Century Library Leader: A Review of Library Leadership Training, 1998–2013." Atlanta, GA: Educopia Institute.

Weiner, Sharon Gray. 2003. "Leadership of Academic Libraries: A Literature Review." *Education Libraries* 26, no. 2: 5–19.

Young, Arthur P., Peter Hernon, and Ronald R. Powell. 2006. "Attributes of Academic Library Leadership: An Exploratory Study of some Gen-Xers." *The Journal of Academic Librarianship* 5, no. 32: 489–502. doi: 10.1016/j.acalib.2006.05.008.

9

Accreditation and Evaluation—Roles for Health Sciences Library Managers

Bethany J. Figg

Key Points

Health sciences library managers serve a critical role in accreditation of organizations when joining self-study committees and volunteering resources to meet accreditation guidelines and requirements.

Health sciences library managers play a key role in the accreditation process of the university, hospital, or medical educational institution in which they work. Accreditation ensures institutions meet the national standards for safety or education or outcomes needed for producing an excellent healthcare workforce and healthy patient outcomes. The institution that accreditation is bestowed upon is seen by colleagues and patients as a sign of competence, excellence, and quality. These institutions are looked to for best practices, networking, and accreditation, which allows them the ability to apply for grant funds and support other educational programming.

The focus of this chapter is on library support and management of the accreditation processes rather than the specific requirements, policies, and agencies responsible for accrediting hospitals, medical schools, and residency training programs. This chapter does not replace the guidelines, manuals, or checklists of accrediting bodies or professional associations, but the library should obtain the guidelines, manuals, and checklists of these entities when assisting with accreditation implementation and accreditation site visits.

The role of the medical librarian in accreditation site visits has evolved over time. Historically, medical librarians either directly or indirectly contributed to 400 of the maximum 1,000 points available to hospitals during a Joint Commission on Accreditation of Healthcare Organizations (JCAHO) site review (Gilliland 1956). Prior to 1987, JCAHO listed health sciences librarians and library services in seven different chapters of their *Comprehensive Accreditation Manual for Hospitals* (Joint Commission on Accreditation of Healthcare Organizations 1988; Schardt 1998). In 1987, JCAHO initiated a major revision in the evaluation process for hospitals, shifting the emphasis away from standards for individual departments to standards for hospital-wide functions. This resulted in the elimination of the "Professional Library Services" chapter from the manual in 1994 (Joint Commission on Accreditation of Healthcare Organizations 1996; Paradise 2004). The 2004 standards moved even further away from a physical library to focus on the functions a library would provide to the hospital. The requirements stated that library services were to be provided in the following manner: If these services were not available on-site, they could be provided by cooperative or contractual arrangements with other institutions (Joint Commission on Accreditation of Healthcare Organizations 2003; Paradise 2004). This effectively made no requirements for the hospital to have a library or a librarian.

On the medical education side of accreditation, health sciences librarians have had an active role in the education of medical students, residents, attending physicians, and other healthcare professionals—yet their medical education accreditation guidelines and standards do not recognize this role (Schwartz et al. 2009). The governing body that renders accreditation decisions on all residency training programs in the United States is the Accreditation Council on Graduate Medical Education (ACGME). The ACGME requires each program to "advance residents' knowledge and practice of the scholarly approach to evidence-based patient care" through activities such as research, grants, quality improvement initiatives, systematic reviews, and review articles (Accreditation Council for Graduate Medical Education 2022a). Yet, no mention is made of the important role librarians serve to meet these standards. Prior to 1999, the standards for residency programs issued by each specialty's residency review committee (RRC) varied greatly regarding libraries. Some RRC standards required access to a library, while others did not mention the need for library services or a professional librarian. In 2006, the Medical Library Association (MLA) sent a letter to the executive director of the Institutional Review Committee of the ACGME requesting an adoption of language requiring an accredited degree-holding librarian and medical library to support graduate medical education programs (Schwartz et al. 2009). While the ACGME did not deny the request outright, they requested the language be more generic since some hospitals may not be able to afford a hospital library. As of 2022, the ACGME Common Program Requirements state that residency programs must provide "access to specialty-specific and other appropriate reference material in print or electronic format. This must include access to electronic medical literature databases with full text capabilities" (Accreditation Council for Graduate Medical Education 2022a). There are no ACGME institutional, common, or specialty-specific requirements requiring a medical library or librarian.

The Liaison Committee on Medical Education (LCME) is the governing body that renders accreditation decisions on all medical schools in the United States and Canada. The LCME has included in their standards for the functions and structure of a medical school a requirement for library resources and staff. According to Standard 5.8, an accredited LCME medical school must provide library resources sufficient to support the educational mission of the medical school and services supervised by professional staff. The requirements do not specify a physical medical library, nor an accredited degree-holding medical librarian (Association of American Medical Colleges and American Medical Association 2022). Due to the lack of support for the medical library and medical librarians in the realm of accreditation, health sciences library managers are required to continue the quest of demonstrating their worth to hospital administration and medical education leaders. This can be achieved by inserting themselves into the accreditation process to assist each school, department, hospital, and clinic to meet or exceed accreditation standards.

Evaluation of the Library

In order to stay relevant in the ever-changing field of health care, health sciences library directors should engage in regular assessment of library needs, preferences, and resources. Reviewing and identifying the library users' needs and interests can allow the library to make incremental changes to services offered and ensure relevancy (Norton et al. 2018). Evaluation of the library should be a 360-degree, multi-sourced assessment that evaluates many aspects of library services. These evaluations could include:

- A survey of the type of technology patrons utilize to access library resources to ensure optimization across devices.
- A technology survey of how patrons utilize their mobile devices to interact with library resources, whether for accessing e-books, journal databases, or shared interactive programs.

- A usage report on point-of-care applications to determine if the products are worth the price.
- Preference for e-books over print books to determine where to devote an appropriate proportion of the library's budget to collection development.
- An exploration of library training services to discover any interest in library classes or workshops on conducting research, how to use presentation tools, information and digital literacy, or mobile device apps for productivity.
- An exploratory survey to find if program leadership would find value in including a medical librarian on rounds in the hospital or as part of a journal club to encourage an evaluation of the medical literature on relevant cases.
- A usage report on the most utilized web pages or resources for medical specialties that could be compiled into a helpful lib guide for quick reference.

It is important for the health sciences library manager to take the information gathered from these evaluations to remove services and resources that are no longer relevant, or implement change, or used. Through a series of surveys averaged over five years, one library found their patrons were less likely to engage with the library on social media (Norton et al. 2018). A response to this trend would be to focus more attention on the medical apps and spend less time adding content to the social media platforms.

Accrediting Bodies

Health sciences library managers may need to engage with a wide variety of accrediting bodies. Some of these institutions accredit the entire hospital, medical school, or residency training sponsoring institution (e.g., Joint Commission, LCME, and/or ACGME), while others accredit programs under the purview of a hospital or healthcare organization (e.g., stroke certification, Primary Care Medical Home, etc.). This section will briefly describe some of the high-level accrediting organizations that health sciences librarians will likely encounter.

- The Joint Commission: The Joint Commission is the nation's oldest and largest standards-setting and accrediting body in health care. Accrediting 22,000 healthcare organizations and programs in the United States, the Joint Commission surveys organizations at least every three years (laboratories are surveyed every two years). Along with accreditation, the Joint Commission also provides certification for programs in these healthcare organizations to include (but not limited to) programs such as stroke, cardiac, palliative care, behavioral health, and Primary Care Medical Home (PCMH) Certification (The Joint Commission 2022).
    - Two smaller organizations are also approved, or receive "deeming authority," by the federal government through the Centers for Medicare and Medicaid Services (CMS) to accredit institutions for CMS payment. These include Det Norske Veritas, Inc. (DNV) and Healthcare Facilities Accreditation Program (HFAP), which accredit a wide range of healthcare organizations such as hospitals (including critical access hospitals and long-term acute care hospitals), ambulatory surgery centers, clinical laboratories, home health, hospice, renal dialysis, and home infusion therapy (Acute Care Hospital Accreditation Program 2022). Approximately 5 percent of healthcare accreditation is done through these two organizations.
- CARF: The Commission on Accreditation of Rehabilitation Facilities is an independent, nonprofit accreditor of health and human services in areas of aging services, behavioral health, child and youth services, employment and community services, vision rehabilitation services, medical rehabilitation, and opioid treatment. CARF accredits more than 60,000 programs and services at over 28,000 locations (The Commission on Accreditation of Rehabilitation Facilities 2022).
- NABP: National Association of Boards of Pharmacy was established to assist the state boards of pharmacy in creating uniform education and licensure standards. The NABP helps support

patient and prescription drug safety, through examinations that assess pharmacist competency, pharmacist licensure transfer and verification services, and various pharmacy accreditation programs (National Association of Boards of Pharmacy 2022).
- ACGME: The Accreditation Council for Graduate Medical Education is the accrediting body for sponsoring institutions, residency training, and fellowship training programs. The ACGME strives to improve patient care delivered by resident and fellow physicians today, as well as in their future independent practice in clinical learning environments characterized by excellence in care, safety, and professionalism (Accreditation Council for Graduate Medical Education 2022b).
- LCME: The Liaison Committee on Medical Education accredits United States and Canadian medical schools through a voluntary, peer-reviewed process of quality assurance that determines whether the medical education program meets established standards. A majority of state licensing boards require graduates of US medical schools to be accredited by the LCME as a condition for licensure (Liaison Committee on Medical Education 2022).
- CODA: The Commission on Dental Accreditation accredits dental and dental-related education programs, including advanced dental education programs and allied dental education programs in the United States (Commission on Dental Accreditation 2022a).
- CPME: The Council on Podiatric Medical Education is the accrediting body for podiatric medical education programs. CPME also provides the recognition of specialty certifying boards for podiatric medical practice (Council on Podiatric Medical Education 2022a).
- CCNE: The Commission on Collegiate Nursing Education assesses and identifies programs engaging in effective educational practices to promote the quality and integrity of baccalaureate, graduate, and residency/fellowship programs in nursing. CCNE accreditation supports and encourages continuous quality improvement in nursing education and nurse residency/fellowship programs (Commission on Collegiate Nursing Education 2022).
- NLN CNEA: The National League for Nursing Commission for Nursing Education Accreditation accredits practical/vocational, diploma (RN), associate, bachelor, master's, clinical doctorate, post-graduate certificate, and distance learning programs to promote excellence and integrity in nursing education globally. The accreditation process respects the diversity of program mission, curricula, students, and faculty; emphasizes a culture of continuous quality improvement; and influences the preparation of a caring and skilled nursing workforce (The National League for Nursing Commission for Nursing Education Accreditation 2022).
- ANCC: The American Nurses Credentialing Center accredits organizations providing nursing continuing professional development and interprofessional continuing education. These accredited organizations help provide nurses with the knowledge and skills to help improve care and patient outcomes (American Nurses Credentialing Center 2022).
- ACCME: The Accreditation Council for Continuing Medical Education accredits organizations providing continuing medical education for physicians. The ACCME does not accredit individual educational activities but the organizations that offer continuing medical education, setting standards for education to accelerate learning, change, and growth in health care (The Accreditation Council for Continuing Medical Education 2022).

Accreditation Evaluation

Accreditation is not a onetime event—policies and procedures must be in place to continually ensure high quality is achieved in these programs. Waiting for a notice of an accreditation site visit to start implementing changes may result in bad outcomes and does not meet the spirit of accreditation purposes (Ajidahun 2020). Utilizing requirements to set systems up correctly, staying up to date on changes and new requirements, and implementing review reports to enact change and improvement are all parts of this process.

Table 9.1. Crosswalk

Program Requirement	2014	2016	Action Plan
VI.A.1.a).(1).(b)	The program director must be committed to and responsible for promoting patient safety and resident well-being in a supportive educational environment.	The program director must design and maintain a program that has a structure that promotes interprofessional team-based care and a culture that provides safe patient care in a supportive educational environment.	Online modules
VI.B.2.b)	The learning objectives of the program must not be compromised by excessive reliance on residents to fulfill non-physician service obligations.	The learning objectives of the program must be accomplished without excessive reliance on residents to fulfill non-physician obligations.	Ensure full medical assistant support for non-physician tasks

What is the librarian's role? The medical librarian can aid with finding the accreditation regulations, rules, and laws. Once these are identified, the librarian can also create a crosswalk from previous sets of requirements to identify new areas or changes from prior years. An example is provided in Table 9.1. Other helpful documents a librarian could find for an accreditation team are articles written by organizations that achieved successful accreditation, lectures online, or accreditation management systems to help maintain accreditation.

Librarians can evaluate the submission records from a prior site review to utilize the self-study documentation and accreditation report for reporting areas to address, highlight, or update based on current accreditation guidelines that may have changed since the prior visit. Leadership teams appreciate dashboards quickly identifying areas meeting accreditation, areas close to not meeting accreditation, and areas not meeting accreditation. A simple "red light, yellow light, green light" dashboard can help leadership focus on a concerning area that should be addressed immediately. An example is provided in Table 9.2.

Table 9.2. Accreditation Dashboard

American College of Surgeons Trauma Accreditation Requirements—Level 1	Meeting Accreditation (Green Light)	Close to Not Meeting Accreditation (Yellow Light)	Not Meeting Accreditation (Red Light)
Board-Certified Trauma Medical Director	Physician on staff		
Two Board-Certified Pediatric Surgeons		Two physicians on staff; one is near retirement	
Board-Certified Neurosurgeon			Do not have; need to hire

Familiarity with all the accreditation associations for a librarian's institution can provide an opportunity for library service promotion. Identifying books, journals, and services supporting curriculum or scholarly activity requirements could be provided to leadership as materials to report to accreditors. Linking library information and data services to satisfy requirements for the area's patient population can be invaluable. Conducting a needs assessment can provide the data needed for leadership to obtain additional staff and resources for the institution (Rand and Gluck 2001). These activities bring awareness to resources the library provides to support and strengthen the organization—not just to meet accreditation standards. This is a short list of ways the medical librarian can assist with an accreditation review, but the librarian will need to express their interest to leadership. Leadership may not immediately think to include medical librarians in their accreditation preparations but volunteering to assist can be a powerful affirmation of the skills and usefulness of the librarian.

Medical library directors can advocate for and provide digital information literacy education to healthcare workers at any stage of medical learning, promoting critical thinking and lifelong learning skills. Many professional health programs emphasize evidence-based practice and a medical education model, which can benefit from library instruction on the information and digital literacy skills to support these activities (Waltz, Moberly, and Carrigan 2020). The medical library can help achieve these goals through teaching digital literacy and the ability to critically appraise medical information and sources found on the internet (Tagge 2018).

Medical librarians should consider professional development to stay current with accrediting body requirements, evaluation of their own institution's accreditation compliance, and methods to assist with a successful site review. Webinars (often free) posted on the accrediting body's website can provide current information on accreditation processes, and some provide methodologies for preparing for and participating in a successful site visit. The librarian can sign up for listservs or e-mail notifications from these accreditation bodies and alert leadership to new requirements or concerns (Rand and Gluck 2001).

Accreditation Preparation

Preparing for a site review and participating in a site visit all can be achieved with the proper tools and planning. While it can be difficult to find accreditation guidelines or standards that directly require library services or a medical librarian, the medical library can meet accreditation standards for adopting evidence-based medicine found in the medical literature, research support, specialty resources, and other information needs. The following are examples of accreditation guidelines with and without library requirements but all where the library can assist with accreditation needs:

- CODA: The Advanced Education in General Dentistry standard 4-1 requires the institution to provide learning resources supporting the program, and more specifically "library resources that include dental resources" (Commission on Dental Accreditation 2022b).
- CPME: The Approval of Podiatric Medicine and Surgery Residencies standard 2.2 requires the institution to afford "access to adequate library resources, including a diverse collection of current podiatric and non-podiatric medical texts and other pertinent reference resources" (Council on Podiatric Medical Education 2022b).
- CCNE: The Accreditation of Baccalaureate and Graduate Nursing Programs standard II-C requires the institution to provide academic support services sufficient to meet program and student needs "which may include library, technology, distance education support, research support" (Commission on Collegiate Nursing Education 2018).
- ACCME: The words library or librarian do not appear in the ACCME Core Accreditation Criteria, but Standard 1 requires all recommendations for patient care in accredited continuing education must be based on current science, evidence, and clinical reasoning (Accreditation Council for Continuing Medical Education 2021).

The medical library director can also assist with more nuanced aspects of the accreditation site visit. Accrediting bodies usually require a self-study report. This self-study requires institutions to look inward at the strengths and weaknesses of their programming. Librarians can offer to serve on the self-study committee to assist with reviewing the self-study report for several reasons:

- Checking for spelling, grammar, and formatting errors can help clean up a report that might otherwise signal a site visitor of carelessness and make them look more closely for mistakes. If a report is not important enough to clean up spelling errors, what else is the institution not being careful with?
- Looking for areas where the library could support an accreditation initiative could be added to the self-study report. Resources to support requirements for information literacy, scholarly activity, curriculum, and other educational components could be highlighted in the self-study as strengths of the program.
- Encouraging a solution to any "weaknesses" in the self-study will show the site visitor the reported weakness is not a fatal flaw to close a program or institution. It is important to be able to identify areas for improvement, but providing a solution—even one that will take years to implement—shows self-awareness and self-improvement.
- Including a sustainability plan for "strengths" can show the site visitors the institution is thinking long-term. The current state may be substantial, but savvy self-study writers will include markers put in place to ensure steady or upward trajectory. While these are not solutions the medical librarian can or should create, bringing these ideas to the self-study committee and helping identify suggested examples help them craft and/or strengthen a self-study report.

During an accreditation site visit, the reviewers often ask for copious amounts of documentation. The librarian can curate a digital library of necessary information to have ready during a review. Full-text resources with practice guidelines, benchmark data, quality and research projects, scholarly activity reports, policies and procedures, and curriculum can all be part of the digital library to be displayed during the site visit.

Scholarly activity is often a requirement for medical institutions and specifically for the educational accreditation for nursing, medical, dental, pharmaceutical, and podiatric students, and training physicians. Librarians can help prepare and maintain accreditation requirements for scholarly activity by providing robust educational programming on library research resources and information literacy objectives (Ma, Stahl, and Knotts 2018). A simple but helpful task for librarians is the ability to find PubMed-indexed articles written by the institution's faculty. Faculty might not keep their professional resumes/curriculum vitae updated with this information, and the site review may require a listing of scholarly work by faculty members. Accrediting bodies may ask for a list of documents identifying research, grant activity, quality improvement projects, and publication references showing proof of the institutions' efforts to advance medicine. Finding these publications, online resources, or scholarly work done by those in the institution and compiling them for the site visitor can help prevent citations that might be issued by the accrediting organization in light of deficiencies.

Perhaps even more useful is for the medical librarian to assist in the ongoing goal of publishing scholarly activity. Copy-editing services are helpful to those both with and without writing experience. Offering workshops or one-on-one sessions to teach students, residents, and attending physicians to conduct a medical literature search can assist with getting their scholarly project started. Coordinating a Writing Accountability Group (WAG) to reserve a specific time and place to ensure progress on scholarly work may help build healthy habits toward writing and project completion (Skarupski and Foucher 2018). Lib guides are able to move the medical library from a library-centered focus to a learner-centered focus by generating subject guides at the point of need (Neves and Dooley 2011). Creating lib guides to promote scholarly activity may include:

- How and where to submit journal articles;
- Creating a visually pleasing infographic or poster for presenting a project;
- Identifying like journals for specific topics;
- Conducting literature searches; and/or
- Checklists to ensure all elements of a publication are included (i.e., for case reports, clinical trials, quality improvement studies, review articles).

Due to versatility and the ability to research, librarians do not have to be limited to one type of accreditation site visit. Serving a wide variety of healthcare workers has always been the role of health sciences librarians, and aiding with sharing knowledge of multi-disciplinary accreditation requirements follows suit.

Accreditation Results

Accreditation site visit results can be labeled many ways but can largely be described with a few terms:

- Initial accreditation: Initial accreditation can also be called pre-accreditation, contingent accreditation, or provisional accreditation. All describe a newly established entity seeking accreditation. Some accreditation visits occur before the program starts, some take place shortly after starting, and some require both types of successful visits. This announces to interested parties the program does not yet have any outcomes and the accredited body is watching closely to ensure compliance and sustainability.
- Full accreditation: Full accreditation may also be called accreditation, continued accreditation, or continued recognition. This takes place when a program is in substantial compliance with the guidelines and requirements set forth by the accrediting body. Full accreditation may include citations and areas for improvement (AFIs) or areas of non-compliance but is still considered a safe environment for health care or learning to take place.
- Probation: Probation may also be called accreditation with warning or administrative probation. Probation means a serious lack of compliance has been identified. This could be for missing required resources, failure to submit mandatory documentation, or the identification of an egregious safety concern. While the program or institution remains fully accredited, it will need to show substantial changes to prevent the probation from turning into a withdrawal of accreditation.
- Withdrawal of accreditation: Withdrawal of accreditation may also be called withdrawal of recognition, accreditation withheld, or accreditation inactive. This status is conferred when a program no longer has the infrastructure and resources to treat patients or teach learners safely.

Some accrediting bodies add qualifiers such as "commendation" for excellent programs consistently meeting requirements above expectations. Others add levels of accreditation (e.g., Level 1, Level 2, Level 3) to denote age or advancement of a program. Once the site visit report has been issued to the organization, discussing the results—both good and bad—is critical to the success of the institution. The commendations should be spread far and wide to engage positive morale with the workers that made it possible. The areas for improvement can be opportunities to engage executive leadership in process improvement and obtain needed resources to support positive accreditation outcomes. Results from an accreditation site visit should be utilized to enact change. For example, accreditation results indicating the need for or the creation of information literacy initiatives in curriculum could be the onus for medical librarians to insert themselves into organizational planning and educational programming (Saunders 2008).

Accreditation requires continuous assessment of resources and evaluation to be maintained. This chapter focused on the role of the medical librarian to prepare for accreditation reviews for the institutions it supports, as well as additional accreditation-related areas the medical librarian can support.

Formal assessment from stakeholders and self-evaluation of library resources can determine how the library meets and helps accreditation efforts. Disappointingly, most healthcare-accrediting bodies do not include a requirement for a qualified health sciences librarian. Taking a proactive role in seeking ways to contribute to meeting accreditation standards can ensure the recognition of the medical library and librarian's importance. If the medical library director does not offer to help with accreditation and evaluation of the accreditation process, leadership may not think to ask for their help.

Discussion Questions

1. How can the librarian utilize accreditation guidelines and recommendations to promote their resources and procure additional support?
2. How can the librarian promote resources that support accreditation initiatives to enhance leadership awareness?
3. If the librarian does not volunteer to assist with the accreditation process, how will leadership know they have the knowledge and resources to assist?

Recommended Readings

Bangert, Stephanie Rogers, and Bonnie Gratch. 1995. "Every Librarian a Leader: Accreditation: Opportunities for Library Leadership." *College & Research Libraries News* 56, no. 10: 697–700. https://doi.org/10.5860/crln.56.10.697.

Blandy, Susan Griswold. 1992. "The Librarians' Role in Academic Assessment and Accreditation." *The Reference Librarian* 17, no. 38: 69–87.

Norton, Hannah F., Michele R. Tennant, Mary E. Edwards, and Ariel Pomputius. 2018. "Use of Annual Surveying to Identify Technology Trends and Improve Service Provision." *Journal of the Medical Library Association* 106, no. 3. http://jmla.pitt.edu/ojs/jmla/article/view/324.

Sacks, Patricia Ann, and Sara Lou Whildin. 1994. *Preparing for Accreditation: A Handbook for Academic Librarians.* Reed Business Information.

References

Accreditation Council for Continuing Medical Education. 2021. "Accreditation Requirements." https://www.accme.org/sites/default/files/2021-12/626_20211221_Accreditation_Requirements.pdf.

Accreditation Council for Graduate Medical Education. 2022a. "Common Program Requirements."

———. 2022b. "What We Do." Accreditation Council for Graduate Medical Education. 2022. https://www.acgme.org/what-we-do/overview/.

Acute Care Hospital Accreditation Program. 2022. "About Us." ACHC. 2022. https://www.hfap.org/about/.

Ajidahun, Clement Olujide. 2020. "Accreditation of Academic Programmes in Adekunle Ajasin University, Nigeria: A Librarian's Perspective." *Mousaion: South African Journal of Information Studies* 37, no. 4. https://doi.org/10.25159/2663-659X/6411.

American Nurses Credentialing Center. 2022. "ANCC Accreditation." ANCC. 2022. https://www.nursingworld.org/organizational-programs/accreditation/.

Association of American Medical Colleges and American Medical Association. 2022. *Functions and Structure of a Medical School: Standards for Accreditation of Medical Education Programs Leading to the MD Degree.* https://lcme.org/publications/.

Bangert, Stephanie Rogers, and Bonnie Gratch. 1995. "Every Librarian a Leader: Accreditation: Opportunities for Library Leadership." *College & Research Libraries News* 56, no. 10: 697–700. https://doi.org/10.5860/crln.56.10.697.

The Commission on Accreditation of Rehabilitation Facilities. 2022. "Who We Are." CARF: The Commission on Accreditation of Rehabilitation Facilities. http://www.carf.org/About/WhoWeAre/.

Commission on Collegiate Nursing Education. 2018. "Standards for Accreditation of Baccalaureate and Graduate Nursing Programs." https://www.aacnnursing.org/Portals/42/CCNE/PDF/Standards-Final-2018.pdf.

———. 2022. "CCNE: Who We Are." AACN: American Association of Colleges of Nursing. 2022. https://www.aacnnursing.org/CCNE-Accreditation/Who-We-Are.

Commission on Dental Accreditation. 2022a. "About CODA." CODA Commission on Dental Accreditation. 2022. https://coda.ada.org/.

———. 2022b. "Advanced Education General Dentistry Standards." https://coda.ada.org/-/media/project/ada-organization/ada/coda/files/advanced_education_general_dentistry_standards.pdf?rev=3be44cd93b824f188b252883455fa8e2&hash=784ECC31337596DE94C16C07666658B9.

Council on Podiatric Medical Education. 2022a. "About the Council." CPME Council on Podiatric Medical Education. 2022. https://www.cpme.org/about/content.cfm?ItemNumber=2427&navItemNumber=2239.

———. 2022b. "CPME 320, Standards and Requirements for Approval of Podiatric Medicine and Surgery Residencies." https://www.cpme.org/files/CPME/2022-4_CPME_320.pdf.

Gilliland, Dabney. 1956. "The Medical Record Librarian: Her Role in Hospital Accreditation." *Hospital Management* 82, no. 5: 86, 88.

The Joint Commission. 2022. "Facts About the Joint Commission." The Joint Commission. https://www.jointcommission.org/who-we-are/facts-about-the-joint-commission/.

Joint Commission on Accreditation of Healthcare Organizations. 1988. *Comprehensive Accreditation Manual for Hospitals: The Official Handbook*. Chicago, IL.

———. 1996. *Comprehensive Accreditation Manual for Hospitals: The Official Handbook*. Chicago, IL.

———. 2003. *Comprehensive Accreditation Manual for Hospitals: The Official Handbook*. Oak Book, IL.

Liaison Committee on Medical Education. 2022. "About." LCME. 2022. https://lcme.org/about/.

Ma, Jinxuan, Lynne Stahl, and Erica Knotts. 2018. "Emerging Roles of Health Information Professionals for Library and Information Science Curriculum Development: A Scoping Review." *Journal of the Medical Library Association* 106, no. 4. http://jmla.pitt.edu/ojs/jmla/article/view/354.

National Association of Boards of Pharmacy. 2022. "About." NABP National Association of Boards of Pharmacy. 2022. https://nabp.pharmacy/about/.

The National League for Nursing Commission for Nursing Education Accreditation. 2022. "NLN CNEA: About." NLN CNEA: The National League for Nursing Commission for Nursing Education Accreditation. https://cnea.nln.org/about.

Neves, Karen, and Sarah Jane Dooley. 2011. "Using LibGuides to Offer Library Service to Undergraduate Medical Students Based on the Case-Oriented Problem-Solving Curriculum Model." *Journal of the Medical Library Association* 99, no. 1: 94–97.

Norton, Hannah F., Michele R. Tennant, Mary E. Edwards, and Ariel Pomputius. 2018. "Use of Annual Surveying to Identify Technology Trends and Improve Service Provision." *Journal of the Medical Library Association* 106, no. 3. http://jmla.pitt.edu/ojs/jmla/article/view/324.

Paradise, Andrew. 2004. "Why the Joint Commission on Accreditation of Healthcare Organizations Should Add New Regulations Regarding Libraries." *Journal of the Medical Library Association* 92, no. 2: 166–68.

Rand, Debra C., and Jeannine Cyr Gluck. 2001. "Proactive Roles for Librarians in the JCAHO Accreditation Process." *Journal of Hospital Librarianship* 1, no. 1: 25–40.

Saunders, Laura. 2008. "Perspectives on Accreditation and Information Literacy as Reflected in the Literature of Library and Information Science." *The Journal of Academic Librarianship* 34, no. 4: 305–13. https://doi.org/10.1016/j.acalib.2008.05.003.

Schardt, Connie M. 1998. "Going beyond Information Management: Using the Comprehensive Accreditation Manual for Hospitals to Promote Knowledge-Based Information Services." *Bull Med Libr Assoc.* 86, no. 4: 504–507.

Schwartz, Diane G., Paul M. Blobaum, Jean P. Shipman, Linda Garr Markwell, and Joanne Gard Marshall. 2009. "The Health Sciences Librarian in Medical Education: A Vital Pathways Project Task Force." *Journal of the Medical Library Association: JMLA* 97, no. 4: 280–84. https://doi.org/10.3163/1536-5050.97.4.012.

Skarupski, Kimberly A., and Kharma C. Foucher. 2018. "Writing Accountability Groups (WAGs): A Tool to Help Junior Faculty Members Build Sustainable Writing Habits." *The Journal of Faculty Development* 32, no. 3: 1–8.

Tagge, Natalie. 2018. "Leveraging Accreditation to Integrate Sustainable Information Literacy Instruction into the Medical School Curriculum." *Journal of the Medical Library Association* 106, no. 3. https://doi.org/10.5195/jmla.2018.276.

Waltz, Micah J., Heather K. Moberly, and Esther E. Carrigan. 2020. "Identifying Information Literacy Skills and Behaviors in the Curricular Competencies of Health Professions." *Journal of the Medical Library Association* 108, no. 3. http://jmla.pitt.edu/ojs/jmla/article/view/833.

10

Managing the Small Health Sciences Library

Priscilla L. Stephenson

Managing a small health sciences library with only one or two librarians and one or two support staff is a typical arrangement for hospital, specialty clinic, federal agency, and association libraries. In many cases, the librarian manages without additional help of any sort—a solo librarian. Librarians in small libraries become adept at multi-tasking and prioritization as they coordinate a full range of library services. While librarians in larger libraries may develop specialized interests and skills, librarians in small health sciences libraries must be able to provide all of the library's services: database searches, interlibrary loans, document delivery, collection development, and instruction, to name just a few basic library operations. In addition to being skilled in all these areas, these librarians must also excel in self-management and be comfortable with rapid changes to the daily schedule. A request for several articles or a literature search will take priority over whatever plans for cataloging or book selection had been on the librarian's day planner!

Key Points

- Librarians in solo and other small health sciences libraries provide hands-on management of daily activities—reference, interlibrary loan, collection management, and library instruction services.
- Look for ways to include useful tallies of completed work while finishing these daily tasks.
- Multi-tasking and flexible planning are needed for successful small library management.

Introduction

In addition to discussing basic business management practices for librarians in small health sciences libraries, this chapter will also review specific management approaches to support the library's basic services: Reference, Document Delivery/Interlibrary Loan, Collection Development, and Instruction.

Managing the Small Department in a Larger Institution

Small libraries are often unique departments in their facilities. Hospital libraries, for example, are among the few non-clinical departments in their facilities working with clinical staff. This lends itself to various management arrangements linking small departments to other small departments in an organizational structure. In a hospital, for example, the library may report to an administrator in departments such as Nursing, Research, Education, or Medicine. In some cases, the library will be the singular "outlier" among departments representing similar employee areas, or the librarian may be one of several smaller departments grouped together with an administrator not affiliated with any of these areas. In either case, it is important to work with your peers, support your supervisor's goals, and network with everyone. Other members of this team may need to learn what a library can—and cannot—do to help the hospital or campus meet institutional goals.

Probably the most important job requirements for the manager of a small library are the ability to prioritize work and to manage time. This is most critical for solo librarians who lack staff to cover for absences or time away from the front desk. New search requests take priority, and if the administrator requests a copy of the newspaper article mentioned on the morning news, there will be no time to finish the book order or resume other tasks planned for the day until the search is complete. Librarians in small libraries must be flexible with their schedules and be ready to pivot as needed. "Time management involves not only simple strategic measures such as prioritizing a to-do list and building gaps in the daily schedule to accommodate unexpected interruptions, but also managing the best use of time" (Solomon 2017, 105).

Personnel Management

For the manager of a small health sciences library, with only volunteer staff to manage, personnel management may not be a major concern beyond daily scheduling. Others with even a few employed library staff members will need to manage annual performance evaluations and comply with requirements regarding timecards, leave balances, hiring regulations, and so on. Compliance with these will often be regulated by legal rulings; be sure to seek out local human resources staff for clarification whenever needed. Most facilities provide an abundance of supervisory training that should be helpful for the intentional learner.

Budget Planning Responsibilities

Planning and monitoring the department budget is an important task for managers of libraries of any size. When the time comes, be sure you are prepared to meet with the facility's fiscal officers to defend your projected budget for the following fiscal year. This budget defense will likely occur months before the end of the current fiscal year, requiring you to research projected price increases from major vendors and to assess your purchase needs before you have firm data. Conduct potential product trials long before you need to determine next year's purchases in all areas of the library's operations—equipment, software, e-book or e-journal collections, and databases. It is to your advantage to utilize multiple-year contracts when feasible. Hopefully your facility will provide contracting staff to support your work and to provide the legal expertise for these arrangements.

For the budget defense meeting, your CFO or other fiscal staff will no doubt provide forms for you to complete prior to that meeting. Review the past one to three years' itemized expenses to check that you've included all recurring purchases in your projections. Be sure you have collected the relevant usage data to support your request to continue a subscription or to cancel one product in favor of another. If you anticipate an objection to a major purchase, solicit letters of support from key leaders in your facility—come to the meeting prepared with answers.

Measurement of Library Usage

Good fiscal management requires the librarian to evaluate both services and resources. Take the time to collect usage and collection data. For usage statistics, consider how users contact you—telephone, e-mail, chat, web page, and face-to-face visits are measurable and will provide useful data, but only if you collect and document it. If you have a walk-in library, add an inexpensive door counter to provide objective data no one can dispute. An alternative suggestion might be to monitor walk-in users for a sample month, making tally marks on your desktop for each new person who enters your library. E-mail service requests can be easily managed and tallied by filtering incoming messages into folders, and counters on web pages can record visits and searches. Statistics should be recorded monthly in a spreadsheet for reporting. At least annually, the library manager should use these statistics to prepare a more visual report for management to demonstrate usage trends over time. A report showing three to five years should provide a useful trend line.

Usage data will demonstrate whether individual databases show evidence of the product's value for the students, faculty, or researchers. Circulation reports provide evidence that library patrons borrow books, download journal articles, and make photocopies from library resources. Tallying statistics and presenting them in a relevant and useful format can be time-consuming, so the manager of a small library needs to be selective in choosing which resources to measure. It may be that the library's online journal or database vendor will provide usage statistics, leaving the library manager to assess more local issues, such as the number of walk-in visitors or whether instruction session attendees found the training valuable. Electronic databases or e-journals will likely be the largest portion of your library materials budget, making the regular review of usage statistics a priority task for the library manager. A single year's data is a good start, but when you can demonstrate a trend over time, your supervisors can be more supportive of your request for continuing or additional funds. Most vendors now provide direct online access to usage data for the library's database administrator, and all of them will provide that information on request.

Statistics documenting the usage of library resources provide important evidence of the library's value to the facility, and they should be shared with the library's supervisor and the campus administration.

Library Assessment and Evaluation

Libraries take evaluation seriously. An annual user survey can assess services and collect users' suggestions. It might be as simple as adding a link requesting service comments in your e-mail signature file, or you might send a brief survey to a specific user group (perhaps internal medicine residents or nurse educators) asking about a particular topic, such as asking them to rate their satisfaction with the library's online journal titles or document delivery service. If you are evaluating a new database, invite a select group of possible users to test the products and ask for their impressions. Involve the library's users in purchase decisions whenever feasible.

If you have time, consider conducting a more detailed evaluation of your library's value. Return-on-investment (ROI) studies are helpful in justifying the costs of sustaining the library's operation and its space commitment. Medical library calculators aim to create objective measures of library value to support their departments to fiscal administrators. These studies use expense data such as salaries for users and librarians, book and journal costs, and research time to develop formulas to calculate library return on investment (Bodycomb and Del Baglivo 2012; Jemison et al. 2009; Kelly, Hamasu, and Jones 2012).

There have been many studies assessing library value. The most well-known is Joanne Marshall's 1992 Rochester Study, which reported on her research of medical libraries' impact on clinical decision-making. In this study, 80 percent of the responding physicians stated that libraries had had a positive impact on their clinical decisions and that "they probably or definitely handled some aspect of patient care differently than they would have handled it otherwise" (Marshall 1992, 169). Other studies of value provided by health sciences libraries include those by King (1987), Fischer and Reel (1992), and Bayrer et al. (2014). In a series of three studies of library reference services conducted in federal medical libraries in 2011, 2014, and 2017, 95 percent (or greater) of the users rated librarians' reference searches positively (Taylor and Stephenson 2018). Some studies focused on specific areas of library practice, such as the link between library searches and length of stay and patient care costs (Klein et al. 1994) and the relationship between library support and morning report (Banks et al. 2007). Kelly et al. commented on the superior value of library assessment and evaluation studies over simple usage data reports:

While recording hash marks to count outputs has long been a standard practice in libraries, identifying and then collecting data that can be used to demonstrate value is much more difficult. One must articulate both the library's goals and the metrics that will describe how library programs achieve those goals. This assessment process and eventual evaluation of the program must be integral to the library and be seen as essential by all staff. Collecting irrelevant data or filing rich data away in a drawer or computer file is simply a waste of time. But regularly collecting the right data, analyzing it, and formally reporting the findings can create a picture of the library as a vibrant, relevant, and irreplaceable resource. (Kelly, Hamasu, and Jones 2012, 657)

Managing Reference and Research Support

For most health sciences libraries, the priority task is to support research. This is true no matter whether the facility is a hospital with a patient care focus, or if it is a research institute where laboratories perform basic science investigations. Research and reference service is the library's principal service and is its justification for continued budget and management support. For the solo librarian, this means that incoming research requests should be managed as priority work tasks. This can be difficult when there are multiple searches and other work requests competing for the librarian's time, but maintaining a flexible schedule will help to meet multiple deadlines.

An important part of reference management is to maintain regular communication with the patron, beginning with an immediate acknowledgment of each new request. For uncomplicated requests, the goal should be to provide the answer—a database search or article—within the same business day. More difficult questions may require more time to search multiple databases, check textbooks, or trace references found in relevant articles. When the search takes more time than expected, the librarian should keep the patron informed, while still delivering each completed project within a few days' time.

Maintaining a record of reference work in progress—and completed—is important for successful management of all the library's tasks. The log of search requests can be a lifesaver for a busy librarian trying to manage and remember multiple tasks, and having a list of completed work will provide statistical data for management reports. Beyond tracking the topic and databases consulted, it may be useful to track the time required to complete each request, especially if library users are involved in systematic or scoping reviews that typically require increased assistance from the librarian. A log of reference requests can also be helpful when determining if there are subject gaps in the book, journal, or database collections to support user needs and research trends.

Managing Interlibrary Loans and Document Delivery

Interlibrary loans and document delivery go hand-in-hand with reference and research support. Most health sciences libraries rely on DOCLINE and OCLC to obtain articles not available locally. It is important to maintain logs of these requests for compliance with Copyright Guidelines and the "rule of five" (American Library Association 1994, 2016; Bernfeld 2006; CCC 2021; Kristof and Mak n.d.). There continue to be questions about the interpretations of the Guidelines (Atwater-Singer and Kristof 2022; Oakley, Quilter, and Benson 2020), but a careful librarian will be mindful of the legal guidelines regarding copies of published (or audio) materials. If a particular title's subscription cost is beyond the library's budget but is critical to the needs of local researchers, the library will need to use the Copyright Clearance Center (copyright.com) to maintain legal compliance for excessive copies of a current title. If the interlibrary loan request includes the actual borrowing or lending of a hard copy, it is critical to maintain an accurate log of the due date and to document when the item is mailed and received. The record-keeping effort can be tiresome, but the loss of a borrowed text can result in an expensive lost book replacement fee and a pile of unwanted paperwork!

Each PubMed citation has a unique identification number, or PMID (PubMed Identifier). DOCLINE (docline.gov) uses the PMIDs as input data for interlibrary loan requests for specific articles, and it matches the PMIDs to the journal holdings records for each participating library. Each DOCLINE library creates a routing table of preferred lenders, and new requests are sent to libraries holding those specific issues. The result is an efficient system that can result in same-day receipt of requested items when libraries remain alert to incoming requests. Like PubMed, DOCLINE is a no-charge service from the National Network of Libraries of Medicine, although lending libraries may charge each other for providing the copies. Multiple no-charge reciprocal borrowing groups exist to provide networks of lending libraries where participating libraries can minimize borrowing costs. Payment to lending libraries can be made conveniently through deposit accounts in the Electronic Fund Transfer System (EFTS) (https://www.mlanet.org/EFTS), a program currently managed by the MLA. Participation in EFTS eliminates the need for libraries to make multiple individual payments for borrowed interlibrary loans, saving valuable accounting time and expense.

As a measure of their customer service efficiency, managers will likely want to report how quickly they receive items borrowed from other libraries. DOCLINE and OCLC (www.oclc.org) provide rapid electronic transmission of requests, and medical sciences libraries now regularly order and receive items the same day. As a result, the library's speedy receipt of interlibrary loan requests should be a strong service measure in the library's management reports. The linking of PubMed citations' unique PMID numbers to the specific journal holdings of participating DOCLINE libraries makes it possible for the system to transmit article requests more efficiently than OCLC for most health sciences journal article requests. However, OCLC remains an important secondary resource for articles outside the normal scope of clinical medicine (e.g., business management or social services), as well as for book loans and requests for chapter copies.

Document delivery in this chapter refers to in-house copies prepared by the library staff and delivered to the patron. This may mean photocopied pages from print books or journals, or it may refer to PDF articles downloaded from online journals. In either case, the librarian needs to maintain a log of these copies for management reports. Because the library has subscriptions to these books and journals, individual article photocopies prepared by library staff are not a copyright concern, unless forbidden by vendor contract. However, such photocopies or downloads by library staff do represent a measure of completed work. Some libraries may include them in circulation counts, just as they tally in-house book circulation. Monitoring the use of subscribed titles is important in assessing the value of the journals for local library users and in making renewal decisions.

Managing Collection Development

Books

Medical libraries have traditionally maintained selective core collections of health sciences reference books to provide subject coverage for a broad range of medical specialties.

Alfred N. Brandon, Director of the Welch Medical Library, was the originator of the "Selected List of Books and Journals for the Small Medical Library," first published in 1965 (Brandon). The scope of the list evolved over time. It came to be known as the Brandon-Hill list, which was used by hospital libraries as a selection and evaluation tool until it ceased publication in 2003. Doody's Core Titles (www.doody.com/dct/) was developed to fill the gap created by the loss of the Brandon-Hill list, and today it serves as a book selection guide for the health sciences (Shedlock and Walton 2006). Certain specialties and professional groups have developed their own recommended book lists. An example is the AACP's triennial list of resources for pharmacy education, developed by pharmacy librarians' reviews and selections (AACP 2021).

For individual print book purchases, it is usually more cost-effective and efficient to use large book vendors (e.g., Rittenhouse Book Distributors, Matthews Book Company, or Complete Book & Media Supply) than to deal with the publishers directly. Amazon may be an option for you as well, depending on your institution's purchasing policy. Electronic titles are often purchased in collections from vendors such as EBSCO, Rittenhouse R2, Ovid, or STAT!Ref. Licensing plans vary from title to title, so examine your purchase options carefully. Are you actually paying for an annual subscription, or is it a one-time purchase? How many concurrent users will be able to read the book at one time? Vendor sales of both print and electronic books occur frequently; work with your vendor representatives to learn about their coming sales dates.

Library catalogs provide a means of maintaining an inventory of library holdings for the library manager. For users, catalogs serve as finding aids to locate a particular title or topic. Library catalogs have long since evolved from wooden drawers of paper cards to online databases of varying complexity. At the far end of the spectrum are the intricate integrated library systems (ILS) that will track a book from purchase request to the shelf and then to checkout for patron use. There are far less complicated commercial systems designed specifically for small libraries, which will meet the inventory and circulation control needs of most small health sciences libraries with limited print titles. For the smallest collections of print materials, a simple spreadsheet listing of books may suffice.

For electronic materials, commercial A-to-Z list software, link resolvers, and discovery services effectively catalog library resources while allowing users to use "Google-like" searches to link to actual book or journal content. Most libraries today rely on "copy cataloging" using sites such as the NLM Catalog (https://www.ncbi.nlm.nih.gov/nlmcatalog) or OCLC's WorldCat (https://www.worldcat.org/). The NLM Classification (https://classification.nlm.nih.gov/) system helps group books on similar health sciences subjects (e.g., laboratory testing) both for the shelf arrangement of physical books and for searchable subject lists of the entire collection. Catalogers also use MeSH (Medical Subject Headings) to assign subject terms to further define the subject content of a given book or journal.

Databases

Because of the emphasis on providing reference services and research support, databases are an important collection expense in health sciences libraries today. Libraries supporting clinical facilities will subscribe to primary literature databases such as PubMed, CINAHL, and PsycINFO. Those with larger budgets and information needs may add Embase, Scopus, or Web of Science as well as specialty products such as pharmacy databases (Micromedex or Lexicomp), additional nursing databases (e.g., Emcare or Joanna Briggs), or mental health resources (e.g., Psychiatry Online or Mental Measurements Yearbook). They may also subscribe to point-of-care tools such as DynaMed, UpToDate, or VisualDx and products combining e-books with special features, such as Clinical Skills or AccessMedicine.

There are new products every year, and successful librarians will be those who stay in touch with industry news to provide the best product options for your library patrons. Database vendors are always ready to demonstrate and promote their products, and vendor exhibits at professional meetings such as MLA and regional chapter events provide important opportunities to see live demonstrations of new products and enlarge your network of vendor representatives. Use mail lists such as MEDLIB-L or the numerous MLA Caucus mail lists to ask your peers about potential product choices you are considering. You may want to request product trials to share with your local users to gauge their opinions and to collect data to support a purchase request.

Journals

Journals are critical in health sciences collections because they contain peer-reviewed reports of the most current medical research. Hospital libraries can manage with smaller collections of core titles and a more limited set of archived backfiles than their university counterparts. Smaller specialized research libraries, such as might be found in university chemistry departments or in a medical society's headquarters, will need more focused but deeper collections to support their specialties. The days of multi-floor shelving for bound periodicals covering fifty-plus years of archival backfiles are gone for all but the largest university libraries. Like their academic health sciences library counterparts, today's small health sciences libraries in hospitals and research agencies have moved to electronic journal collections, as funds permit. Current journal subscriptions in these libraries are generally limited to titles not available online, unless there is strong support for walk-in library users, such as students or patients.

The shift to e-journals means that certain journal management tasks are no longer needed, such as check-in of individual issues, claiming missed issues, duplicate exchange, shelving print issues, and article photocopying. These tasks are replaced, however, by far more complicated technical tasks to ensure continued and uninterrupted access to the local server, internet network, and publishers' sites. These require frequent communication with a variety of IT support personnel in the librarian's home facility as well as at the publisher or journal vendor sites. The first indication of an access problem will no doubt come from a local user unable to log in to a specific journal issue, making this an immediate customer service priority for the library staff.

Electronic journal subscriptions are generally more expensive than their print equivalents, and they are often purchased in publishers' packaged collections (e.g., JAMA Network, Elsevier's Science-Direct) or database aggregators (e.g., EBSCO, Ovid, ProQuest). Tools for managing e-journals include products to permit secure remote access (e.g., OpenAthens or EZproxy) and link resolvers to support full-text linking (e.g., 360Core, 360Link). PubMed's Outside Tool (formerly LinkOut) is a full-text link resolver for PubMed citations, and Third Iron's LibKey and LibKey Nomad will link a library's specific journal holdings to full-text articles.

Managing Library Instruction

Instruction is an important component of library service, especially to support an electronic collection of books, journals, and databases. Librarians become accustomed to coping with individual publishers' various download instructions, but library users are often infrequent users of online services and need more guidance to find the library's list of online resources, run effective searches, and download articles for use. Even if the library has a physical space with print resources, virtual training options should be used for off-shift staff and those working in off-site clinic locations. Because everyone has a preferred learning style, library training options should include a variety of approaches, including short lunch-and-learn sessions, one-on-one scheduled search help sessions, and scheduled online vendor training programs. Whenever possible, provide hands-on training so that the learners can successfully locate information from the library's resources during the class. Explore training options provided by other departments in the facility. Do educators provide large in-person auditorium sessions? Do they use Zoom, Teams, or Webex? Prepare handouts, videos, web page aids such as LibGuides, and PowerPoint training aids for those who want to review the procedures after the live events. If time permits, scheduled chat sessions can provide training options. Vendors utilize YouTube channels for database training, and many will provide online database training to supplement programs for newcomers to your facility, such as faculty, residents, or nursing students.

Marketing and Advocacy

The growth of virtual libraries has created a need for new marketing techniques. Managers need to market library resources and services even more assertively and frequently when users cannot see books on display or browse new journal issues on the shelves. Users need to know when and where to find the library, how to use it, what resources it provides, how to access library services, and how to use databases effectively. Create bookmarks for walk-in visitors and a single-page handout describing library services. If there is a face-to-face orientation for new students or employees, provide a handout or e-mail message with the library's URL or SharePoint address.

Marketing needs to be frequent and varied to reach library users in numerous ways. Options might include blast e-mail messages to target groups, flyers in the cafeteria, and campus electronic bulletin boards. To improve your ability to market quickly, develop a template for e-mail messages and

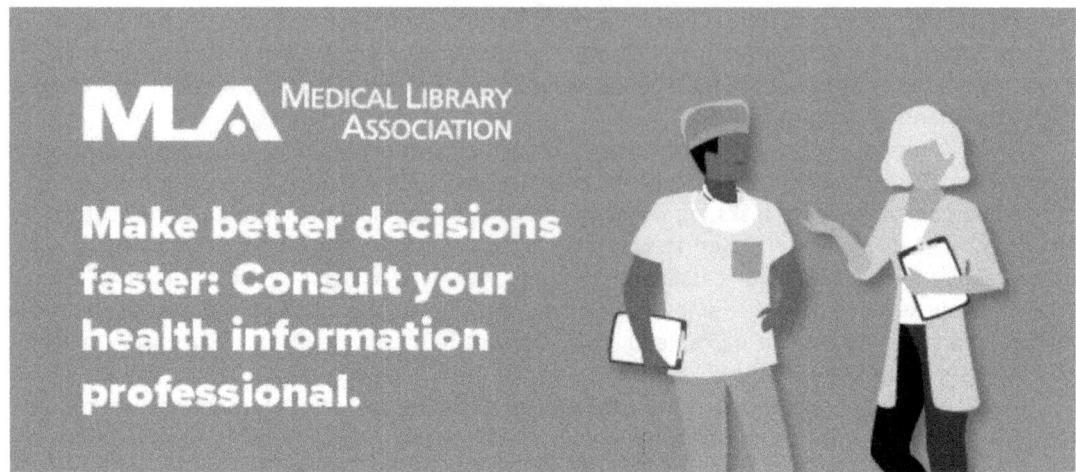

Figure 10.1. Medical Library Association e-mail marketing image.
Reprinted with permission from the Medical Library Association, 2023.

small flyers that will provide a visual identity for library messages. Create an e-mail signature file that promotes the library's online site, physical location, new book lists, or other important news. Celebrate campus events such as Nurses' Week or Research Day by preparing a list of new books of interest to those groups. Use marketing materials provided by other groups, such as MLA's annual posters and bookmarks to promote National Medical Librarians Month each October. Figure 10.1 illustrates an MLA image to use in an e-mail signature file.

Advocate for the library's resources and services by being a regular attendee at facility committee meetings for groups with obvious library connections—research, accreditation, and education committees are all possibilities. These committees allow the librarian to network with peers in other departments and to advocate for the library in hospital or campus activities. Have a marketing plan that includes a schedule of classes, demos, e-mails, and/or a library newsletter—keep it varied but regular. Prepare the often-mentioned "elevator talk" to have relevant good news stories ready to share with library visitors (Corcoran 2018). A nurse supervisor will want to know more about your work when you say, "We are working with the evidence-based nursing task force on their new project." And the Medical Department Chair will be happy to hear about a new cardiology book collection. Do not let your good news be a secret! "You can have $1M worth of resources, but if no one knows about them or how to use them, what you've got doesn't matter" (Peterson 2019).

Managing Library Space

Library space is often in highly desired campus locations, no matter the setting. New academic or clinical programs may dictate a need for a redesign of available space, and the library manager may be told about a coming space reduction with relatively short notice. With the growth of online journals, fewer visitors come to the library to browse the shelves to check the new journal issues or new print book titles. If the library has discarded bound periodicals after purchasing the titles online, there remains highly visible empty shelving that attracts the envious eyes of other departments. A best practices approach would be to plan ahead and prepare to replace the empty shelving with a redesigned space that accommodates changing needs for additional computers or study rooms. All too often, library space is lost to another department, either partially or completely. A 2022 survey of pediatric hospital librarians found that 14 percent (nine in sixty-three) no longer had any physical library space (Willis et al. 2023).

Conclusion

This chapter has focused on the tasks and responsibilities of management in the small health sciences library. Some of these libraries will be solo operations where there is a single library manager who must be there to open and close the library each day, providing all the services needed to support information services to the library's patrons. In other settings, the librarian will have one or more assistant staff members and will have more flexibility to participate in clinical rounds or other library-related tasks outside the library's doors. Even with an additional one or two staff assistants, the library's basic responsibilities will continue to fall on the manager's shoulders, such as answering reference questions, filling document orders, managing electronic resources, purchasing books, journals, and databases, and instructing users about the most efficient uses of online library products. Small medical libraries are usually busy places, where the workday is never boring because of the variety of daily work. However, the position can elicit high stress levels as the librarian juggles competing priorities in a limited number of work hours. Librarians need to adapt to future needs to keep their libraries viable and important to the future of their institutions. "[I]ncreased demand from library users in the health sciences environment forces solo librarians or staff in small libraries to transform in order to remain relevant" (Solomon and Muir 2017, 111).

Discussion Questions

1. What key survey question for library users would you ask as a link from your e-mail signature file? Which service or resource do you want users to evaluate with this survey question?
2. Are there advantages to purchasing an online journal *collection* containing 80 percent of the titles you need (and 20 percent of only minimally relevant titles) versus purchasing only the specific *individual* titles your library needs?
3. How does PubMed support access to full-text articles?
4. Which new databases do you hope to purchase in the next fiscal year and why?

Recommended Readings

Evans, G. Edward, and Stacey Greenwell. 2020. *Management Basics for Information Professionals*, 4th ed. Chicago, IL: Neal-Schuman.

Health Sciences Librarianship. 2014. Edited by M. Sandra Wood. Lanham, MD: Rowman & Littlefield.

References

American Association of Colleges of Pharmacy (AACP). 2021. *AACP Basic Resources for Pharmacy Education*. Winter Edition. Editors: Jason Guy, PharmD and Ivan Portillo. https://connect.aacp.org/viewdocument/aacp-basic-resources-for-pharmacy-e-4.

American Library Association. Reference and User Services Association (RUSA). 1994, 2016. *Interlibrary Loan Code for the United States*. 1994, revised 2001, 2008, 2015, and 2016. https://www.ala.org/rusa/guidelines/interlibrary.

Atwater-Singer, Meg. and Cindy Kristof. 2022. "The Persistence of CONTU: The Results of Two Surveys." *OCLC RSC22 Web Series*. https://www.oclc.org/en/events/confererences/resource-sharing-conference/2022.html.

Banks, Daniel E., Runhua Shi, Donna T. Timm, Kerri Ann Christopher, David C. Duggar, Marianne Comegys, and Jerry McLarty. 2007. "Decreased Hospital Length of Stay Associated with Presentation of Cases at Morning Report with Librarian Support." *Journal of the Medical Library Association* 95, no. 4: 381–87. doi: 10.3163/1536-5050.95.4.381.

Bayrer, Rebecca, Suzanne Beattie, Elizabeth Lucas, Dawn Melberg, and Eve Melton. 2014. "What Have We Done for You Lately? Measuring Hospital Libraries' Contribution to Care Quality." *Journal of Hospital Librarianship* 14, no. 3: 243–49. doi:10.1080/15323269.2014.888514.

Bernfeld, Betsy A. 2006. "Free to Photocopy? A Legislative History of Section 108, the Library Photocopying Provision of the Copyright Act of 1976." *Legal Reference Services Quarterly* 25, nos. 2–3: 1–49.

Bodycomb, Aphrodite, and Megan Del Baglivo. 2012. "Using an Automated Tool to Calculate Return on Investment and Cost Benefit Figures for Resources: The Health Sciences and Human Services Library Experience." *Journal of the Medical Library Association* 100, no. 2: 127–30. doi: 10.3163/1536-5050.100.2.011.

Brandon, Alfred N. 1965. "Selected List of Books and Journals for the Small Medical Library." *Bulletin of the Medical Library Association* 53, no. 3: 329–64.

Copyright Clearance Center (CCC). 2021. "Interlibrary Loan Copyright Guidelines and Best Practices." https://www.copyright.com/wp-content/uploads/2015/03/White_Paper_ILL-Brochure.pdf.

Corcoran, Kate E. 2018. "National Medical Librarians' Month—What's Your Story?" *MLA New Members Blog*. Accessed July 20, 2023. https://www.mlanet.org/p/bl/ar/blogaid=1720.

Fischer, Wenda W., and Linda B. Reel. 1992. "Total Quality Management (TQM) in a Hospital Library— Identifying Service Benchmarks." *Bulletin of the Medical Library Association* 80, no. 4: 347–52.

Jemison, Kay, Edward Poletti, Janet Schneider, Nancy Clark, and Ron Drew Stone. 2009. "Measuring Return on Investment in VA Libraries." *Journal of Hospital Librarianship* 9, no. 4: 379–90. doi:10.1080/15323260903253803.

Kelly, Betsy, Claire Hamasu, and Barb Jones. 2012. "Applying Return on Investment (ROI) in Libraries." *Journal of Library Administration* 52: 656–71. doi: 10.1080/01930826.2012.747383.

King, David N. 1987. "The Contribution of Hospital Library Information Services to Clinical Care— A Study in Eight Hospitals." *Bulletin of the Medical Library Association* 75, no. 4: 291–301.

Klein, Michele S., Faith Van Toll Ross, Deborah L. Adams, and Carole M. Gilbert. 1994. "Effect of Online Literature Searching on Length of Stay and Patient-Care Costs." *Academic Medicine* 69, no. 6: 489–95. doi: 10.1097/00001888-199406000-00017.

Kristof, Cindy, and Collette Mak. n.d. "Copyright and Libraries: Resource Sharing." In *Legal Issues in Libraries and Archives, an Open Textbook for Library and Information Science Courses,* edited by Ruth Dukelow and Michael Robak. Minnesota Libraries Publishing Project. Creative Commons 4.0. https://mlpp.pressbooks.pub/librarylaw/chapter/copyright-ill/.

Marshall, Joanne G. 1992. "The Impact of the Hospital Library on Clinical Decision Making: The Rochester Study." *Bulletin of the Medical Library Association* 80, no. 2: 169–78.

The Medical Library Association Guide to Managing Health Care Libraries, 2nd ed. 2011. Edited by Margaret Moylan Bandy and Rosalind Farnham Dudden. New York: Neal-Schuman.

Moran, Barbara B., and Claudia J. Morner. 2018. *Library and Information Center Management,* 9th ed. Santa Barbara, CA: Libraries Unlimited, ABC-CLIO.

Oakley, Meg, Laura Quilter, and Sara Benson. August 31, 2020. "Modern Interlibrary Loan Practices: Moving Beyond the CONTU Guidelines, an ARL White Paper." *Association of Research Libraries.* https://doi.org/10.29242/report.contu2020.

Peterson, Jonna. 2019. "Get to Know: Jonna Peterson, MLIS." *BMJ Insider's Quarterly Newsletter.* https://bmjinsiders.com/tag/clinical-informationist/.

Shedlock, James, and Linda J. Walton. 2006. "Developing a Virtual Community for Health Sciences Library Book Selection: Doody's Core Titles." *Journal of the Medical Library Association* 94, no. 1: 61–6.

Solomon, Meredith, and Meghan Muir. 2017. "Solo Librarians." In *Transforming Medical Library Staff for the Twenty-First Century*, editors Melanie J. Norton and Nathan Rupp, 103–14. Lanham, MD: Rowman & Littlefield.

Taylor, Mary Virginia, and Priscilla L. Stephenson. 2018. "Demonstrating Value in Federal Medical Center Libraries" *Medical Reference Services Quarterly* 37, no. 4: 403–12. doi:10.1080/02763869.2018.1514914.

Transforming Medical Library Staff for the Twenty-First Century. 2017. Edited by Melanie J. Norton and Nathan Rupp. Lanham, MD: Rowman & Littlefield.

Willis, Christine, Kate Daniels, Brian L. Baker, Claudia M. Schuchardt-Peet, Amy Six-Means, and Priscilla L. Stephenson. 2023. "Assessment of Library Services in Pediatric Hospitals in the United States and Canada." Presentation Medical Library Association, Detroit, MI. May 17, 2023.

Index

Page references for figures are italicized.

AACP Basic Resources for Pharmacy Education, 101
AAHSL (Association of Academic Health Sciences Libraries), 7
AAMLA (African American Medical Librarians Alliance/MLA) Mentoring Program, 70
academic libraries cf. hospital and special libraries, 2
accessibility considerations, 29;
    accessibility standards for virtual and physical spaces, 30
    Braille signage and markings, 30
    diverse dietary needs of staff, 31
    gender-neutral restrooms, 30
    gender-neutral signage, 30
    lactation rooms, 30
    ACCME (Accreditation Council for Continuing Medical Education), 88, 90
    ACGME (The Accreditation Council for Graduate Medical Education), 86, 88
ACRL (Association of College and Research Libraries) Harvard Leadership Institute, 7
advocacy for library, 104;
    class schedule, 104
    demonstrations, 104
    elevator talk, 104
    facility committees, 104
    newsletter, 104
Age Discrimination in Employment Act of 1967 (ADEA), 27
American Indian Library Association (AILA), 23
Americans with Disabilities Act of 1990 (ADA), 27
ANCC (American Nurses Credentialing Center), 90
Asian/Pacific American Librarians Association (APALA), 23
ARL (Association of Research Libraries), 23
ARL (Association of Research Libraries) Leadership and Career Development Fellows Program, 7, 70
assessment and evaluation:
    circulation data, 98
    document delivery log, 101
    interlibrary loans log, 100
    library usage data, 98
    library value studies, 99
    medical library calculators, 99
    ROI (return on investment) calculators, 99
    search log, 100

belonging, 17
BIPOC (black, indigenous, and people of color), 21, 23-26
Black Caucus of the American Library Association (BCALA), 23
book collection (electronic), 102;
    AccessMedicine, 102
    EBSCO, 102
    Ovid, 102
    Rittenhouse R2, 102
    STAT!Ref, 102
book collection (print), 101;
    Brandon-Hill list, 101
    Doody's Core Titles, 101
budget planning, 98

career mapping, 64
CARF (Commission on Accreditation of Rehabilitation Facilities), 87
CCNE (Commission on Collegiate Nursing Education), 88, 90
Chinese American Librarians Association (CALA), 23
Civil Rights Act of 1991, 27
Clifton StrengthsFinder, 5
collection development, 97, 101;
    electronic book purchases, 102
    print book purchases, 101
CODA (Commission on Dental Accreditation), 88, 90
Copyright Clearance Center, 100

Copyright Guidelines, 100
conflict avoidance, 39
CPME (Council on Podiatric Medical Education), 90
critical conversations, 25

databases, 98;
    AccessMedicine, 102
    CINAHL, 102
    Clinical Skills, 102
    DynaMed, 102
    EMBASE, 102
    Emcare, 102
    Joanna Briggs, 102
    Lexicomp, 102
    management, 102
    Mental Measurements Yearbook, 102
    Micromedex, 102
    Psychiatry Online, 102
    PsycINFO, 102
    PubMed, 102
    SCOPUS, 102
    usage measurement, 98
    UpToDate, 102
    VisualDx, 102
    Web of Science, 102
DEI (Diversity, Equity, and Inclusion), 5, 27, 29
DEIB (Diversity, Equity, Inclusion, Belonging), 15-31;
    assessing DEIB, 21
    normalized pronouns, 30
DISC personality assessment, 5
diversity, 17, 25
DOCLINE, 100
    routing table, 101
document delivery services, 97, 101
    document delivery logs, 101

Electronic Fund Transfer System (EFTS), 101
electronic journal collections, 103
    Elsevier Science-Direct, 103
    JAMA Network, 103
electronic titles:
    360Core, 103
    360Link, 103
    A-Z lists, 102
    discovery services, 102
    LibKey (Third Iron), 103
    LibKey Nomad (Third Iron), 103
    link resolvers, 102
    management, 102, 103
    Outside Tool (PubMed), 103

emotional intelligence, 54
empathy, 27
Equal Pay Act of 1963 (EPA), 27
equality, 17
equity, 17

Family and Medical Leave Act of 1993 (FMLA), 27

gender wage gap, 22
Genetic Information Nondiscrimination Act of 2008 (GINA), 27

hospital libraries, 97
    organizational structure, 97

ILS (integrated library system), 102
implicit biases, 18
inclusion and inclusivity, 16, 17
individual development plan, 62
Innovative Leadership Institute, 69
institutional awareness, 5
interlibrary loan services, 97, 100

JCAHO (Joint Commission on Accreditation of Hospitals), 10, 85
Joint Commission, 10, 87
journal collection management, 102

LCME (Liaison Committee on Medical Education), 88
Leadership:
    contingency, 53
    servant, 53
    situational, 53
    transformational, 53
library assessment and evaluation, 99
library catalogs, 102
library instruction, 97, 103
library leaders' responsibilities, 1
    budget planning, 6
    delegation of duties, 6
    fiscal management, 6
    leading staff, 4
    peer networking, 6
    political awareness, 2, 3
    strategic planning, 2, 4
    support for larger organization, 3, 4
    team building, 5
library space management, 104
licensing electronic titles, 102
lifelong learning, 28

mail lists, 102
marketing, 103
   email marketing image, *104*
   marketing methods, 103
   marketing plan, 104
   National Medical Librarians Month, 104
MEDLIB-I, 102
mentoring: 57, 61
   communication consistency, 65
   diversity and inclusion in mentoring, 67
   effective mentoring, 65
   matching mentors and mentees, 69
   mentee tips, 65
   mentor selection, 67
   mentor tips, 65
   mentor-mentee relationship, 62
   mentoring benefits, 64
   mentoring challenges, 66, 67
   mentoring circles, 63
   mentoring moments, 64
mentorship program:
   commitment to mentorship program, 69
   mentorship program closure, 69
   mentorship program culture, 69
   mentorship program goals, 68, 69
mentoring, stages:
   closure, 62
   enabling growth, 62
   negotiation, 62
   preparation, 62
mentoring, types:
   collaborative/group, 63
   distance/virtual, 63
   flash, 63
   formal, 63
   informal, 63
   mentoring types, chart, *68*
   one-on-one, 63
   peer, 63
   reverse, 63
   team, 63
MeSH (Medical Subject Headings), 102
Minnesota Institute (The Minnesota Institute for Early Career Librarians from Traditionally Underrepresented Groups), 71
MLA (Medical Library Association), 17
   MLA Competencies for Lifelong Learning and Professional Success, 37
   MLA Competency 4: Leadership and Management, 54-56
   MLA email marketing image, 104

MLA (Medical Library Association) Mentoring Program, 71
MLA Reads, 28
MLA Rising Star Program, 71
Myers-Briggs Type Indicator (MBTI), 5

National Association of Librarians of Color, 23
NABP (National Association of Boards of Pharmacy), 87
National Network of Libraries of Medicine, 101
NLM Catalog, 102
NLM Classification, 102
NLM (National Library of Medicine), 7
NLM/AAHSL (National Library of Medicine/ Association of Academic Health Sciences Libraries), 71
NLM/AAHSL Leadership Fellows Program, 57, 59

OCLC, 101

pay transparency legislation, 37
performative diversity, 29
personnel:
   management, 98
   recruitment and retention, 6, 21-22
   recruitment strategies, 23
   retention strategies, 24
   salary inequity, 22
   stay interviews, 25
PMID (PubMed Identifier), 100
political awareness, 2,3
Pregnancy Discrimination Act of 1978 (PDA), 27
privilege, 18
professional development of staff, 24, 65
psychological safety, 26

reference and research services, 97, 100
patron communication, 100
prioritization, 100

quiet quitting, 36

REFORMA: National Association to Promote Library and Information Services to Latinos and the Spanish Speaking, 23
Rehabilitation Act of 1973, 27
reliability and consistency, 66
remote access:
   EZProxy, 103
   OpenAthens, 103
rule of five, 100

schedule flexibility, 98
self-awareness, 18
self-reflection, 21
setting limits and boundaries, 66
SHRM (Society of Human Resource Management), 17
soft skills, 54
strategic planning, 2, 65

time audit, 57
time management, 98
Title VII of the Civil Rights Act of 1964, 27
Title IX of the Education Amendment of 1972, 27

VA (Department of Veterans Affairs) Mentorship Program, 71
vocational awe, 21, 37

About the Editors

Claire B. Joseph has over thirty years of experience in health sciences libraries. She is the Medical Library Director at Mount Sinai South Nassau Hospital in Oceanside, New York. Claire is the author of *The Medical Library Association Guide to Developing Consumer Health Collections*, published by Rowman & Littlefield in 2018, and is the Editor-in-Chief of the *Journal of Consumer Health on the Internet*. Claire continues to be active in Medical Library Association and its Caucuses and Chapters; she has served as Chair of three MLA Caucuses and one MLA Chapter.

Priscilla L. Stephenson was Chief, Library Service for James A. Haley Veterans' Hospital in Tampa, Florida, at the time of her retirement in 2022. During her forty years as a health sciences librarian, she directed both VA and public hospital libraries and served as Head of Reference Services at the University of Tennessee Health Sciences Center Library. She has published and presented at professional library meetings and edited columns for the *Journal of Consumer Health on the Internet* (2002-2022) and *Medical Reference Services Quarterly* (2012-2023). She has been active in the Medical Library Association, serving as Chair of the Continuing Education Committee (2002-2004), the Hospital Libraries Section (2013), the Federal Libraries Section (2009), and the Southern Chapter of MLA (2006). She was awarded MLA's Lois Ann Colaianni Award for Excellence and Achievement in Hospital Librarianship in 2013 and was named a Fellow of the Association in 2019. As a member of the VA Library Network, she served as a mentor to new VA librarians (2017-2022) and was a member of the VA Library Network Advisory Council (2008-2018).

About the Contributors

Melissa De Santis, MLIS, is the director of the Strauss Health Sciences Library at the University of Colorado Anschutz Medical Campus. She has worked in library administration for over fifteen years. Before moving into library administration, Melissa held multiple positions on the public services side of librarianship, including reference, instruction, access services, and library computer labs. Melissa received her MLIS from UCLA and has spent her career in academic health sciences libraries. She is active in several professional associations, including Medical Library Association (MLA) and Association of Academic Health Sciences Library (AAHSL). Her research areas of interest include diversity, equity, and inclusion (DEI) in libraries, scholarly communication, and relationships between academic health sciences libraries and health systems.

Dr. Bethany Figg is currently the Director of Graduate Medical Education for Central Michigan University College of Medicine–CMU Medical Education Partners in Saginaw, Michigan. In her GME role, she utilizes her medical librarian training to research and pursue resources to provide publishing and scholarly activity opportunities for the institution. She also applies these skills and experience to research resources for maintenance of accreditation for her institution and the ten residency and fellowship training programs. She is the Past-President of the Metropolitan Detroit Medical Library Group, Senior Member of the Academy of Health Information Professionals, President-Elect of the Michigan Association for Medical Education, and a column editor for a peer reviewed health sciences library journal. Dr. Figg obtained her doctorate in education technology from Central Michigan University and is an Assistant Professor, Medical Sciences Discipline for the Central Michigan University College of Medicine.

Sandra G. Franklin, MLS, AHIP, FMLA, is director of the Emory University Woodruff Health Sciences Center Library, Atlanta, Georgia. She is a member of the Emory Libraries Senior Management Team and serves on a number of position-relevant committees.

Sandra's service to the Medical Library Association (MLA) includes Board of Directors, National Program & Local Assistance Committees, and chair of MLA's Diversity & Inclusion Task Force. Sandra is a member of several MLA caucuses. Sandra delivered MLA's 2021 Janet Doe Lecture and is an MLA Fellow.

Sandra's service to the Association of Academic Health Sciences Libraries (AAHSL) includes chair of the NLM/AAHSL Future Leadership Committee, Board Member, and President. Sandra was a mentor for the NLM/AAHSL Leadership Fellows Program 2021–2022. She received AAHSL's Gerald J. Oppenheimer Cornerstone Award for service to the profession in November 2022.

Sandra was a 2022–2023 sponsor/mentor for the Association of Research Libraries Leadership and Career Development Program. She is a member of the Friends of the National Library of Medicine Board of Directors and serves as co-chair of the Education Committee.

Shannon D. Jones (she/her) is the Director of Libraries for the Medical University of South Carolina in Charleston. She is also the Director of Region 2 of the Network of the National Library of Medicine. Shannon's educational background includes an Ed.D. in Educational Leadership from Charleston Southern University, an M.Ed. in Adult Learning with a concentration in Human Resources

Development from Virginia Commonwealth University, and a Master of Library Science from North Carolina Central University.

A long-time MLA volunteer, Dr. Jones has served the Association in many capacities, including the 2022-2023 MLA President. During her term as MLA President, she established the Be Well MLA initiative to encourage MLA members to prioritize their wellness and well-being. In 2018, Shannon co-founded the MLA Reads Virtual Book Discussion Club to provide a forum where participants can learn, discuss, and process the implications of various diversity, equity, and inclusion (DEI) topics in their work as information professionals and in their personal lives. Shannon is the co-editor of *Diversity and Inclusion in Libraries: A Call to Action and Strategies for Success* and the forthcoming volume *Cultural Humility in Libraries*.

Dr. Jones' current research focuses on staff recruitment and retention, diversity, equity, inclusion, and belonging (DEIB) in libraries, wellness and well-being for information professionals, and leadership in academic health sciences libraries.

Gerald (Jerry) Perry, MLS, AHIP, FMLA, is Associate Dean for the University of Arizona Libraries (UAL). He serves on the Deans Working Group, which provides executive oversight of UAL. All UAL Research and Learning Liaison Librarians at both the Main and Health Sciences Libraries report to him through their Department Heads. The Director of the HSL is also a direct report. Jerry is responsible for UAL analytics and assessment efforts, has oversight of the User Experience team, and serves as liaison from Administration to the Libraries' Diversity, Social Justice, and Equity Council. Jerry is a member of the faculty at University of Arizona (UA) with continuing status (tenure) at the full librarian rank. He is a past President of the Medical Library Association (MLA) and a Fellow of the Association. He has served as a library professional for nearly forty years, with over forty-five years of total library experience. Academic interests include leadership and administration, informatics, evidence-based practice, and diversity and inclusion.

Katherine "Katie" Prentice, MSIS, AHIP, is Executive Director at the Texas Medical Center Library (TMC Library) in Houston, Texas. She manages library services and information resources for the member institutions of the TMC Library, serving thousands of students, faculty, and researchers. Previously, Katie worked for the University of Oklahoma-Tulsa, Schusterman Library and the University of Texas Health Science Center-San Antonio, Briscoe Library. Her research and management/leadership interests include space use/usability, library assessment, and mentoring for early and mid-career librarians. Katie chose a career in library and information science after serving as a volunteer English language teacher in the Republic of Latvia with the United States Peace Corps. She has a cat named Coco and loves to travel, try new foods, and meet new people.

Gabriel "Gabe" R. Rios, MLIS, is the director of the Ruth Lilly Medical Library, Indiana University School of Medicine. The Indiana University School of Medicine is the largest medical school in the nation and includes nine campuses around the state. Gabe provides vision and strategic leadership for his teams, focusing on education, research, and clinical enterprises of the School of Medicine. His previous position was Deputy Director at the Lister Hill Library, University of Alabama at Birmingham. Gabe has served in administrative roles since 1998 and has worked in several areas of librarianship, including leadership, planning, evaluation, management, organizational dynamics, research services, team building, health literacy, and information technology. Gabe has also served as a member of the MLA Executive Board and as the National Program Committee co-chair for the 2011 MLA meeting. He is an NLM/AAHSL Leadership Fellow from the class of 2003-2004 and served as a mentor for the Leadership Fellows class of 2021-2022.

Tara Douglas-Williams, MSLS, AHIP, is the Associate Director of the Emory University, Woodruff Health Sciences Center Library in Atlanta, Georgia. She holds a master's degree in Library Science from Clark-Atlanta University and received a Bachelor of Science degree in Biology/Natural Sciences from Spelman College. Tara is a 2013-2014 graduate of the AAHSL/NLM Leadership Fellowship Program.

Over the span of her career, Tara has held various positions in academic, hospital, and health sciences libraries. She has been instrumental in the development and implementation of innovative library services and provides effective leadership in transforming service models.

She currently serves on the MLA Board of Directors. She also serves on the Biomedical Informatics, Library and Data Science (BILDS) Review Committee for the National Library of Medicine (NLM). Tara recently completed the 2022 Harvard University Essential Management Skills for Emerging Leaders course.

www.ingramcontent.com/pod-product-compliance
Lightning Source LLC
Chambersburg PA
CBHW081832300426
44116CB00014B/2559